THERE WERE A LOT OF REASONS
FOR SO MANY MILLIONS
TO FALL IN LOVE WITH M*A*S*H

There were the characters—the crazy crew who made the 4077 Mobile Army Surgical Hospital a healing haven of madcap sanity in a world gone too mad to take without strong doses of life-giving laughter.

There were the stories. From the first eye-rubbing episode to the final farewell party that brought tears to eyes from coast to coast. There were quotes. The multitude of marvelous punch lines that scored direct hits on your funny bone and went straight to your heart.

Here at last is the book millions of fans have been waiting for—

M*A*S*H
THE OFFICIAL 4077 QUIZ MANUAL

PAUL BERTLING, television addict and trivia collector, lives in Milwaukee, Wisconsin, with his wife and young son. This is his first book.

M*A*S*H
THE OFFICIAL 4077 QUIZ MANUAL

* * *

PAUL BERTLING

A PLUME BOOK
NEW AMERICAN LIBRARY
NEW YORK AND SCARBOROUGH, ONTARIO

To Dreams.

To Bobi,
For making it through this dream
and a big part of every other.

To Bradley and Alison,
for making yet another reality.

Also Pauline (1932–1981),
Who believed in everything I did.

And for all his advice,
a special thank you to
Chuck Jackson.

LIBRARY OF CONGRESS CATALOGING IN PUBLICATION DATA
Bertling, Paul
  M*A*S*H: the official 4077 quiz manual.
  1. M.A.S.H. (Television program)—Miscellanea.
1. Title. II. Title: MASH.
PN1992.77M2854B46   1984   791.45'72   83-23840
ISBN 0-452-25505-8

PLUME TRADEMARK REG. U.S. PAT. OFF. AND FOREIGN COUNTRIES
REGISTERED TRADEMARK—MARCA REGISTRADA
HECHO EN HARRISONBURG, VA., U.S.A.

SIGNET, SIGNET CLASSIC, MENTOR, PLUME, MERIDIAN
and NAL BOOKS are published *in the United States* by New
American Library, 1633 Broadway, New York, New York
10019, *in Canada* by The New American Library of Canada
Limited, Inc., 81 Mack Avenue, Scarborough, Ontario M1L 1M8

First Printing, April, 1984

2   3   4   5   6   7   8   9

PRINTED IN THE UNITED STATES OF AMERICA

C*O*N*T*E*N*T*S

I∗N∗T∗R∗O∗D∗U∗C∗T∗I∗O∗N

The night of February 28, 1983 will always be remembered as the night *M*A*S*H* made television history by being the most-watched single television show in the industry's history.

An estimated 125 million Americans looked on as the men of the 4077th finally folded their tents and left Korea exactly eleven seasons after they first began.

But no sooner had the final credits flashed across the nation's TV screens than the telephones at both 20th Century-Fox Television and CBS-TV began ringing:

"What was the name of the Mozart piece played by the Chinese prisoners and directed by Major Winchester?"

"Who was the beautiful Korean War Bride Klinger married?"

And the calls haven't ceased.

So for all you *M*A*S*H* trivia buffs out there (and there must be thousands of you judging from the calls and letters we keep getting) here is the definitive book that hopefully will tell you everything you've always wanted to know about *M*A*S*H*—and perhaps a little more.

Now, let's see . . . what was the name of Colonel Potter's horse . . . ?

— Burt Metcalfe
Executive Producer
M∗A∗S∗H

A WORD FROM THE AUTHOR

Attention . . . attention, all personnel: incoming quizzes. Though the 4077 has packed up and gone home, the memories of this Mobile Army Surgical Hospital (M*A*S*H) live on in the pages of this manual.

Follow the madcap crew of surgeons, nurses, and enlisted men— Hawkeye Pierce, Trapper John, Radar O'Reilly, Henry Blake, Frank Burns, Margaret ("Hot Lips") Houlihan, Sherman Potter, B.J. Hunnicut, Charles Emerson Winchester, Father Mulcahy, and Max Klinger—as they cut their way into your funny bone.

Test your recall of the zany sayings and unforgettable situations we've seen over the last eleven years. That is all.

Paul Bertling

THE
Q*U*E*S*T*I*O*N*S

1. THE EASY STUFF

Name the actor or actress who played these members of the 4077.

1. Hawkeye Pierce
2. Trapper John
3. B.J. Hunnicut
4. Frank Burns
5. Col. Potter
6. Henry Blake
7. Radar O'Reilly
8. Charles Emerson Winchester III
9. Margaret Houlihan
10. Nurse Kellye
11. Sgt. Zale
12. Max Klinger
13. Father Mulcahy
14. Rizzo
15. Igor

Seated (l-r): Alan Alda and Wayne Rogers. Standing (l-r): Loretta Swit, Larry Linville, McLean Stevenson and Gary Burghoff

2. IN THE BEGINNING

All these questions have to do with the pilot episode and its transition from the movie. Can you remember that far back?

1. Who was the first actor to play Father Mulcahy?
2. Who was Ho-John?
3. What was Lt. Dish's first name?
4. What was the date of the pilot episode?
5. Who was the original producer?
6. What actor was in the movie and the pilot, but played different characters in each?
7. Was Jamie Farr in the pilot?
8. On what day of the week did the pilot air?
9. Two actors played the same characters in both the movie and the pilot. Name the actors.
10. Who played Ginger, the nurse?

3. CAPT. BENJAMIN FRANKLIN PIERCE, M.D.

1. Where did Hawkeye go to school?
2. What was the name of the book Hawkeye's friend, Tommy Gillis, was writing?
3. What was Hawkeye's first job?
4. Who was the "incredibly average guy" Hawkeye went to med school with?
5. Of what political party is Hawkeye a member?
6. In what city did Hawkeye do his surgical residency?
7. What stopped Hawkeye from getting married?
8. What memory will he take home with him?
9. What did Hawkeye say he would *never* do?
10. Who were the only people Hawkeye ever saluted?

(Right) Alan Alda as Hawkeye

Wayne Rogers as Trapper John

4. CAPT. JOHN McINTYRE, M.D.

1. What did Trapper forget under his bed when he left the 4077?

2. What was Trapper's full name?

3. In what city did Trapper intern?

4. What was wrong with the brown pinstripe suit he had tailor-made?

5. Trapper was in a mine field trying to save a Korean boy. Henry had a map that could help them get out safely. Why was this almost a deadly venture?

6. What was Trapper's shoe size?

7. The supply line was cut. All the officers were assigned duties. What was Trapper in charge of?

8. What was the name of the little Korean boy Trapper was going to adopt?

9. What was Trapper's recipe for martinis?

10. What did Margaret say about Trapper when he and Hawkeye were trying to sober her up under a shower?

5. NICKNAMES

People with nicknames on *M*A*S*H* are as common as the army uniform itself. Try to match the person with the nickname. Some may not have appeared on the show but were only referred to.

1. Gen. Hamilton	a. Boots
2. Col. Houlihan	b. Tippy
3. Gen. Korshak	c. Binky
4. Col. Flagg	d. Boom-Boom
5. Cpl. Miller	e. Iron Guts
6. Col. Fr. Gallagher	f. Howitzer
7. Lt. Brooks	g. Tamer of the Tiger Tank
8. Gen. Kelly	h. Sparky
9. Col. Brighton	i. The Wind
10. Sgt. Pryor	j. Buzz

6. CPL. WALTER O'REILLY

1. What was Radar's middle name?

2. According to Radar, what did he learn to do at the age of four?

3. What was the name of the girl Radar got a "Dear John" record from?

4. Where did Radar get his high school diploma?

5. What religion is Radar?

6. Radar paid $55 for a correspondence course in writing. What was the name of the school offering the course?

7. The school's fee was $50 for materials. What was the other $5 for?

8. How did Hawkeye say good-bye to Radar?

9. What was Radar's disc-jockey name?

10. What three musical instruments did Radar play on the show?

7. LT. COL. HENRY BLAKE, M.D.

1. Where did Henry keep the key to his liquor cabinet?
2. According to Blake, how did he knock the siding off his house?
3. What did Radar see in Henry's ear when he gave Henry a physical?
4. What was Henry's mother's name?
5. What was the most serious meeting Blake had to call?
6. Mrs. Blake had a baby while Henry was in Korea. Was it a boy or a girl?
7. What did Hawkeye, Trapper, and Radar give Henry as a going-away present?
8. What did Blake collect as a child?
9. What was Henry's monthly pay?
10. Where was Henry Blake's plane shot down?

McLean Stevenson as Henry Blake

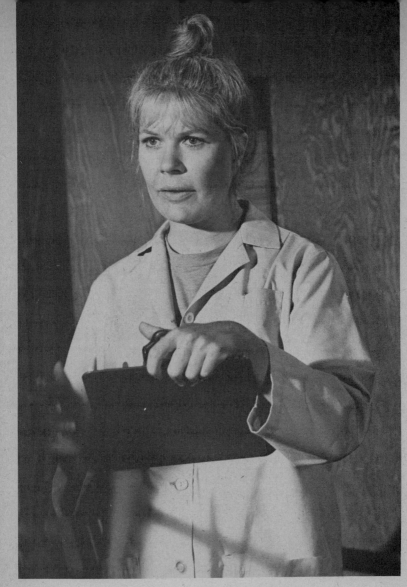

Loretta Swit as "Hot Lips" Houlihan

8. MAJ. MARGARET ("HOT LIPS") HOULIHAN, R.N.

1. Where did Margaret get her wedding dress?
2. Where was she born?
3. How much did Margaret make per month in the army?
4. What were Margaret's husband's outstanding features?
5. What was her husband's name?
6. How long was Margaret in the army before she got married?
7. What did the inscription on her wedding ring say?
8. What did she bring back from Tokyo to unveil on the first day of spring?
9. Where did Margaret get the idea for a time capsule?
10. What were Margaret's requirements for a perfect man?

9. MAJ. FRANK BURNS, M.D.

1. What was Frank's religion?

2. What did Frank always eat on his birthday?

3. Where did Frank get the nickname Ferret Face?

4. What kind of dog did Frank have at home?

5. How did Frank sign his letters to his wife?

6. What were Frank's operating specialties?

7. Frank once made out his will because he thought he was on his deathbed. What did he leave to his "little soldier," Margaret?

8. What was Frank's rank in his medical school graduating class?

9. Frank once received a Purple Heart for being wounded by shell fragments. What was so unusual about that injury?

10. Frank smashed his $14 watch with a hammer. How did this come about?

Larry Linville as Frank Burns

10. THE WARTIME LOVERS

This quiz is about the doctor and nurse who found each other during the cold nights in Korea. Margaret and Frank spent a lot of time together. Can you remember their fond memories?

1. What night of the week was Frank and Margaret's night together?

2. Frank asked Margaret how he rated as a surgeon. What was her reply to him?

3. How could Margaret tell when Frank was double-talking?

4. What did Frank love most about Margaret?

5. What did Margaret tell Hawkeye about Frank's lips?

6. What was the name of this loving couple's polka-dot stuffed dog?

7. In the pilot, what were Frank and Margaret doing the first time we saw them?

8. What did Margaret give Frank on their first anniversary?

9. Frank always shaved before he went to see his "little soldier." Then he sprinkled a little after-shave on himself. What was the name of his after-shave?

10. These two were together, the song "I'm in the Mood for Love" was playing on the record player. Suddenly, Frank's back went out. What did Frank do about his back?

11. HOMETOWNS

This is just a matter of matching the person to his/her hometown.

1.	Capt. Steve Newsome	a.	Mill Valley, California
2.	Sgt. Zale	b.	Toledo, Ohio
3.	Cowboy Hodges	c.	no hometown
4.	Hawkeye	d.	Bridgeport, Connecticut
5.	Frank	e.	Portland, Oregon
6.	Capt. Tuttle	f.	Ottumwa, Iowa
7.	Trapper	g.	Reno, Nevada
8.	Klinger	h.	Baton Rouge, Louisiana
9.	Pvt. Rich	i.	Crabapple Cove, Maine
10.	B.J.	j.	Chicago, Illinois
11.	Henry Blake	k.	Brooklyn, New York
12.	Father Mulcahy	l.	Fort Wayne, Indiana
13.	Margaret	m.	San Antonio, Texas
14.	Rizzo	n.	Honolulu, Hawaii
15.	Dagwood the cat	o.	Boston, Massachusetts
16.	Dr. Paul Yomado	p.	San Francisco, California
17.	Potter	q.	Philadelphia, Pennsylvania
18.	Nurse Kellye	r.	Battle Creek, Michigan
19.	Radar	s.	Bloomington, Illinois
20.	Charles	t.	Hannibal, Missouri

William Christopher as Father Mulcahy

12. FATHER JOHN FRANCIS PATRICK MULCAHY

1. What was the good Father's "given" name?
2. What did Father Mulcahy do to relax?
3. What did he teach before the war?
4. Father Mulcahy ordered Communion wafers from supply. What came instead of the wafers?
5. At Donald Penobscott's stag party, Father Mulcahy made a comment about the last stag party he attended. What did he say happened?
6. Aside from building spiritual morale, what other duties did the Father have?
7. What religious order did Father belong to?
8. What happened to Father Mulcahy just before he left the 4077?
9. What was the name of the division chaplain, Father Mulcahy's superior?
10. What musical instrument did the Father's sister, Sister Angelica, play?

13. CPL. MAXWELL KLINGER

1. On what street corner in Toledo was Klinger's house located?

2. What was the date of Klinger's entrance exam and his first attempt at a Section 8?

3. Why does Klinger want to get a Section 8?

4. What do all the babies in the Klinger family have in common?

5. What was Klinger's original job at the 4077?

6. According to Klinger, there were only three other people who smoked the same cigars he did. Name them.

7. What did Klinger give as his serial number?

8. What was the Klingers' song when they were married?

9. Who was the uncle Klinger wrote to describing all the crazy people he worked with?

10. What was Klinger's religion?

Jamie Farr as Klinger

14. AND YOU THOUGHT WE WEREN'T WATCHING

Compared with most television shows, M*A*S*H has been very consistent in its facts. I should say fairly consistent. There are a few cases where things just didn't coincide with what was said once before. Here are a few of those cases.

1. Radar was discharged because he was the only one who could take care of his mother. In another situation, Radar said he had a brother. What was his brother's job?

2. Potter was at the New Year's Eve party in 1950. Why was this impossible?

3. B.J. said the closest he got to building something was making a bed. Why is that hard to believe?

4. Henry's wife's legs are the subject. He once described her as a thirty-five-year-old bow-legged woman. Yet Radar repeated something else he had said to Hawkeye. What else did Henry say about her legs?

5. Potter said he would retire in Hannibal, Missouri. But he also said he was from another town in Missouri. What town was that?

6. Hawkeye once received a sweater in the mail. He said it was from his sister. Why is this impossible?

7. Margaret once said Henry looked like her deceased father. Why is this hard to believe?

8. The still was described as having a charcoal and sweatsock filter. It was also described as having another kind of filter. What was the other filter made of?

9. Radar saved a lamb from becoming an Easter dinner for some Greek soldiers. He wanted to send it home to his parents. Why was this impossible?

10. Hawkeye said he got his nickname from the only book his father ever read, *The Last of the Mohicans*. Why does this seem hard to believe?

15. PRANKS ON FRANK

Aside from all the clever insults and the constant ribbing, Hawkeye and Trapper pulled a lot of pranks on Frank. This quiz is in two parts. The first part is matching. These are things they said they did to Frank, but we never saw. The second part is actual acts we saw the two crazy doctors pull.

Part I

1. peanut butter
2. ether
3. tonsils
4. an appendix
5. hamburger

a. in his ear
b. in his boot
c. in his other boot
d. in his stethoscope
e. in his after-shave lotion

Part II

1. Put a _____ on Frank while he was drunk.
2. Nailed him in a _____.
3. Trapper _____ in his Bible.
4. _____ while he was in the latrine.
5. Fooled him into buying _____.

16. CAPT. JONATHAN TUTTLE

1. What college did Tuttle graduate from?
2. What were his parents' names?
3. What year was this fine doctor born?
4. What color were his hair and eyes?
5. How did he die?
6. What were his duties at the 4077?
7. Who gave Tuttle's eulogy?
8. What was his religion?
9. Who replaced Tuttle after he died?
10. What actor played Tuttle?

(Above and right) Behind the scenes on the M*A*S*H set

17. BEHIND THE SCENES

This test is designed to find out how carefully you read the credits and cast of characters.

1. What famous actor/director directed fifteen of the first thirty episodes?

2. Who wrote the theme song?

3. Where was *M*A*S*H* filmed?

4. Who cast the show?

5. In the show "Love and War," Hawkeye fell in love with a Korean woman who had lost everything in the war. This was not the working title of the episode. What was?

6. Did Gary Burghoff ever direct any of the shows? Which ones?

7. Who was the medical adviser to the show?

8. Who was the last producer of the show?

9. Who is the author of the original *M*A*S*H* novel?

10. What actress did some writing for and appeared on the show?

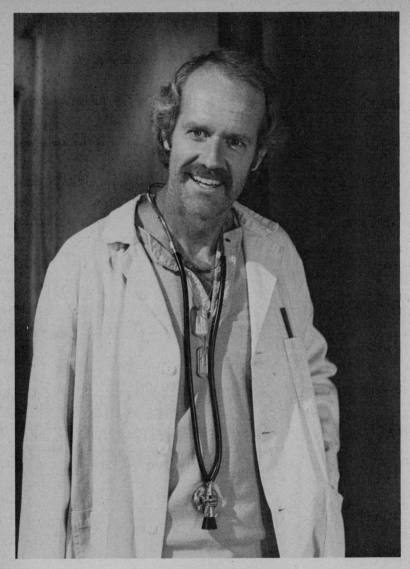

Mike Farrell as B.J. Hunnicut

18. CAPTAIN B.J. HUNNICUT, M.D.

1. What did the initials B.J. stand for?
2. Who was B.J.'s friend and best man at his wedding?
3. What was the first thing B.J. said to Frank?
4. What did he have that reminded him of the "good times"?
5. How did B.J. make Charles think he was losing weight?
6. How many generations of doctors were in B.J.'s family?
7. What did Nurse Donovan have to do with B.J.?
8. Who was B.J.'s favorite comedian?
9. What was the date of the Hunnicuts' wedding anniversary?
10. What was B.J.'s phone number?

Harry Morgan as Col. Potter

19. COL. SHERMAN T. POTTER

1. When Potter heard "Sentimental Journey," who came to his mind?

2. What kind of car did Potter have at home?

3. How did he get his Purple Heart during World War II?

4. What was he allergic to?

5. What seemed to be Potter's favorite saying?

6. What was his favorite meal after church on Sundays?

7. What musical instrument did Mrs. Potter play?

8. Who was the woman Potter almost had an affair with?

9. In the episode in which the 4077 was overrun with Korean orphans, what did Potter read to them as a bedtime story?

10. Where did Potter get his military training?

20. MAJ. CHARLES EMERSON WINCHESTER III, M.D.

1. What musical instrument did Charles play?

2. Being the perfectionist that he was how long did Charles scrub before operating?

3. What was Charles's favorite television cartoon?

4. Charles graduated with two letters in athletics. What were the two sports?

5. What was his religion?

6. What was Charles's class ranking at Harvard?

7. What did Charles like to do to relax?

8. What was his address in Boston?

9. Charles and his sister were four-time champions at what game?

10. In trying to save a soldier's life under sniper attack, what triggered Charles's overwhelming interest in death?

David Ogden Stiers as Winchester

21. MISH-M*A*S*H

This quiz has all the tough-to-remember details.

1. What was the name of the Korean version of Tokyo Rose?
2. What were the tables in the officers' club made of?
3. Aside from Klinger, who else did the enlistment officer, Vickers, talk into reenlisting?
4. What was the name of the newspaper Klinger started for the camp?
5. Where is grape Nehi bottled?
6. Where was the departing lounge for outgoing patients?
7. What was the reason everyone in camp knew everything that happened?
8. What kind of car did Radar's uncle drive?
9. What was the punch line of the joke Hawkeye considered the funniest clean joke ever told?
10. What was the most popular dance at the 4077?

22. OCCUPATIONS

Match the person to his/her occupation or specialty. This may not be as easy as it seems.

1. Hawkeye's father
2. Radar's Uncle Howard
3. Klinger's cousin Num Num
4. B.J.'s father-in-law
5. Henry Blake's brother
6. Klinger's Uncle Amos
7. Meg Cratty
8. Norman Chase
9. Igor's job back home
10. Dr. Borelli

a. makes bird baths
b. runs an orphanage
c. notary public/dance instructor
d. doctor
e. works in a slaughterhouse
f. a roller derby racer
g. veterinarian
h. prison warden
i. medical adviser
j. proctologist

23. COL. FLAGG

1. What was Flagg's trademark?

2. What did Flagg call Col. Potter?

3. What did Flagg want with a dozen scorpions?

4. Hawkeye asked Flagg to find something he had lost twenty years ago. What was it?

5. Flagg called Frank a commie simp. What did he say this meant?

6. According to Flagg, who was he always trying to stop?

7. Why couldn't anyone ever get the truth out of Flagg?

8. Why did Flagg never laugh?

9. What was the colonel's first name?

10. Why did Flagg determine that Frank was a commie just because he was reading the *Reader's Digest?*

Edward Winter as Col. Flagg

24. CELEBRATIONS

The 4077 would celebrate almost anything. Can you recall any of these gala events?

1. Who made the party favors for the Derby Day Bash?

2. How did Henry say he came dressed to the Mardi Gras celebration?

3. Hawkeye and Trapper planned a Thanksgiving party. What was the theme of the party?

4. Who threw Henry's going-away party?

5. On the Fourth of July, Father Mulcahy wanted to have a picnic. He got corn on the cob and all the fixings for the picnic. How did the cook ruin this event?

6. Hawkeye and B.J. planned a crab boil. Klinger went to get all the necessities. Klinger was late and they thought he went AWOL. What took Klinger so long?

7. Hawkeye started a rumor that Marilyn Monroe was coming to the 4077. What was the name Potter gave to the party plans?

8. Home-away-from-home was the theme of a party. What was the party for?

9. Who played Father Time at the New Year's Eve party?

10. Hawkeye took it upon himself to stop the war. When he returned from the peace talks, the 4077 saluted him with a bash. What was so unusual about the party?

25. STRICTLY RELATIVE

Many of the main characters have referred to members of their families. Those references will help you answer this test.

1. What was Mrs. Potter's first name?

2. How many children did Frank Burns have?

3. Charles had one sister. What was her name?

4. What was Margaret's father's full name and rank?

5. Did Trapper John have any children?

6. Name Klinger's father.

7. Did Hawkeye have any brothers or sisters?

8. Name the members of B.J.'s family.

9. What were Col. Blake's children's names?

10. What was Hawkeye's father's first name?

26. DOUBLE TROUBLE (1)

This is a test that will check your recall of specific details. All the questions have two answers. Check your skill in remembering both the answers.

1. B.J. received a book in the mail. The whole camp read this mystery one chapter at a time. (The last chapter was missing so no one knew how it turned out.) What was the author's name and the title of the traveling mystery?

2. Potter decided that the 4077 was out of shape. The camp was expected to participate in the MASH Olympics. B.J. and Hawkeye were the team captains. What were the team names?

3. Potter did many things to keep himself busy while he was off duty. What were his two hobbies?

4. Frank was ordered to operate on a German shepherd. The dog was a member of the U.S. Army. What was his name and rank?

5. B.J. thought it would be a good idea for the members of everyone's family to meet each other, a bit of a 4077 reunion without the guests of honor. After many months of trying to decide where and when it would be held, the party came through. What was the date of the party and where did it take place?

27. THE SWAMP

1. What two pictures did Frank hang in the Swamp?
2. What did B.J. call the still?
3. What type of alcohol was made in the still?
4. According to Hawkeye, what was the model for designing the Swamp?
5. What kind of chair was in the Swamp, right next to the still?
6. What did B.J. want to put in the Swamp to ease the frustration?
7. Where was the dart board?
8. What hung on the center pole?
9. B.J. and Hawkeye made a bar out of Frank's bed. Although it stood only an hour or so, they named the bar. What was the name?
10. What was the last city added to the signpost outside the Swamp?

28. NURSES

1. Whose picture hung in the nurses' tent?

2. What was Nurse Edwina's ("Eddie") last name?

3. Aside from Margaret, what nurse did Frank say he admired?

4. Who was the first nurse Hawkeye could not make love to because of his own physical reasons?

5. Trapper boxed a marine so a certain nurse could remain at the 4077. What was that nurse's name?

6. What did Klinger and Nurse Debbie Clark have to do with each other?

7. Who played Nurse Kellye?

8. Who played Lt. Dish?

9. Nurse Millie Carpenter was killed by stepping on a land mine. Hawkeye read her diary to get some information for her eulogy. What did he find out about Millie?

10. What was Nurse Ginger's last name?

The M*A*S*H nurses as they appear in the show's opening credits

29. I'LL DRINK TO THAT

This test is designed to see if you noticed all the details. Try to match the characters with their favorite drink. Some may have just been referred to.

1. Gen. Clayton
2. Frank Burns
3. Margaret
4. Gen. Mitchell
5. B.J.
6. Radar
7. Charles
8. Potter
9. Lorraine Blake
10. Hawkeye

a. scotch and 7-up
b. gin and tonic
c. grape Nehi
d. sherry and ginger ale
e. bourbon
f. Shirley Temple
g. scotch
h. gin martini
i. cognac
j. rye

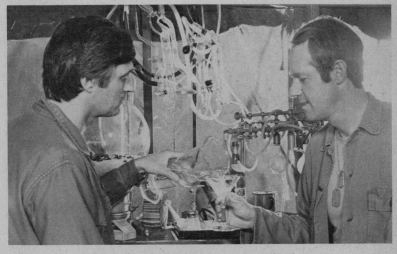

Hawkeye and B.J. enjoy a cocktail.

30. THAT'S ENTERTAINMENT

1. How many USO shows came to the 4077?

2. Klinger worked as a straight man for the announcer/comedian of a USO show. What was the man's name?

3. Radar also participated in one of the shows. What did he do?

4. What was the name of the group of three blondes in blue dresses who sang for a USO show?

5. Potter became good friends with the stripper Brenda Delinski. He caught her show and garter many times in the early years. What was her stage name?

6. Why was one of the shows held over at the 4077 an extra night?

7. Potter and the stripper ended up back at his tent one night. They split a bottle of twelve-year-old scotch. She made a move for him. What happened?

8. Margaret also had a chance to get into the show. What song did she sing?

9. Who caught the stripper's garter?

10. Five people traveled with the show: the comedian; the stripper; Sara, the singer; and two other girls. One girl was in love with Hawkeye, the other was the accordion player. What were their names?

31. WHAT'S IN A NAME?

On occasion, the regular characters referred to a member of their families, or when a character made more than one appearance on the show, two different names were used for the same person. The writers probably thought we weren't watching, but if you were you'll have no problem with this quiz.

1. Potter referred to his grandson as little Skip, but on one occasion he called him something else. What was that other name?

2. Everyone knows that Henry's wife's name was Lorraine. But in the beginning of the series another name was used for his spouse. That name was . . .

3. In one episode Frank was being awarded the Purple Heart. Blake called him Franklin D. Burns. Yet another time Frank had a different middle name that didn't begin with a D. What was that name?

4. When Sidney Freedman first appeared on the show his name was not Sidney. What was it?

5. Hawkeye once said Tommy Gillis had been his best friend since the fourth grade. But when Sidney was examining him, Hawkeye had another person in mind when he talked about his only childhood friend. What was his friend's name?

6. Blake stated that he had only two children, Janey and Andy. In the movie he received from his wife, their daughter was having a birthday party. Her name was not Janey. What was it?

7. Radar referred to his only dog at home as Ranger. On another occasion he called the dog something else. What was the other name?

8. Capt. Halloran came to the 4077 from Army Intelligence. He was played by the same actor who played an all-time favorite. Who was this other character?

9. Either it was a mistake or an oversight, but Radar's mother and their cow had the same name. What was that name?

10. Potter talked about his only child, Evy. But he once said he had a son born in 1926. What was the occupation of this son?

32. WHAT DOES IT SAY ON . . . ?

1. . . . a case of barbecued ribs from Chicago?

2. . . . the door of the OR?

3. . . . Father Mulcahy's sweatshirt?

4. . . . the toe tag Hawkeye put on Frank?

5. . . . an Italian soldier's "Dear John" letter?

6. . . . the side of a chopper?

7. . . . Henry's coffee mug?

8. . . . Klinger's baseball jersey?

9. . . . the fake promotion Hawkeye won for Radar in a poker game?

10. . . . the telegraph Hawkeye sent to Harry Truman?

33. THE KLINGER COLLECTION

Max Klinger, the best-dressed person at the 4077, has a closet full of nice clothes—for both sexes. Do you remember these little numbers?

1. How was Klinger dressed for MacArthur's visit?

2. When was the first time he put the Klinger Collection up for sale?

3. What did he say he once used to make a necklace?

4. What part of his collection did Klinger give to Father Mulcahy so he could keep warm?

5. Klinger was wearing a pink evening gown in a picture. Who did he give that picture to before that person left the 4077?

6. Klinger tried desperately to go AWOL. What gave him away when he was dressed like a Korean woman?

7. What type of dress did Klinger wear to Margaret's wedding?

8. Klinger once dressed as Zoltan. Who was this man with the invisible camel?

9. In the first season, Klinger wore a red scarf around his neck. Who did he get the scarf from?

10. Klinger's bra size was 36B, but what was the brand name he wore?

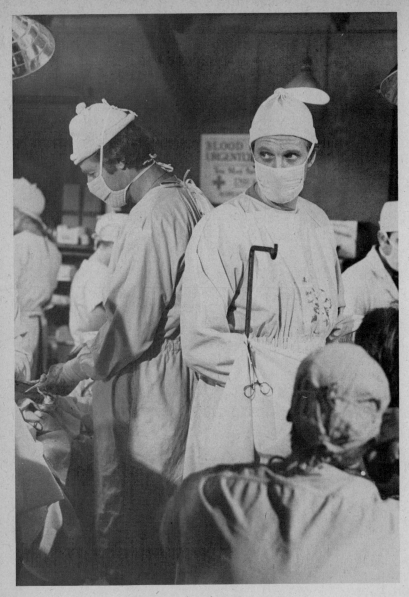

Antics in the operating room

34. THE OPERATING ROOM

1. How many tables were in the OR?

2. Where did patients go after they left the 4077?

3. Mr. and Mrs. Kwan had a baby boy in the 4077's OR. What did the Kwans name their little boy?

4. Why did Radar have to scrub up to assist Margaret at an operation?

5. Hawkeye and B.J. paid $10 to Mr. Shin, the junk dealer, for something he designed for medical use. What was the item?

6. What was the first medical procedure Charles undertook at the 4077?

7. The 4077 needed a kidney machine. Where did they get the parts to make the machine? (They sent away for them, but where?)

8. Margaret once insisted that Charles rescrub. They began to argue. What was it that Margaret said he did to justify rescrubbing?

9. When the laundry bag caught fire, what did Klinger throw on it thinking this would put it out?

10. Henry looked at an X-ray of a soldier. He saw something that shouldn't have been there and that made him think the soldier still had his clothes on. What was it?

35. THE SPORTS PAGE—PAGE ONE

Games and sports were popular diversions at the 4077. See if you can score high on this one.

1. What was the 4077's version of the Kentucky Derby?

2. In a camp football game, why were the Protestants beating the Catholics 7 to 3?

3. What was Double Cracko?

4. While playing volleyball in the Swamp, what did they use for a ball?

5. What were used as jockeys in the roach races?

6. When Charles and Potter were laid up with the mumps, what card game did they play?

7. What game did Hawkeye play as a boy with his father while driving in the car?

8. What was the prize for the winning team of the M*A*S*H Olympics?

9. What was sometimes used as a substitute for darts in the dart board?

10. Norman Polanski's model boat took first prize in the cesspool race. What was the name of his vessel?

36. RADAR'S CRITTERS AND OTHER ANIMALS

Match animals with their names.

1. Radar's female rabbit
2. B.J.'s dog
3. Potter's horse
4. Radar's goat
5. The marine's racing mouse
6. Radar's racing mouse
7. Radar's dog at home
8. Radar's male rabbit
9. Radar's cow at home
10. Radar's female guinea pig

a. Daisy
b. Ranger
c. Edna
d. Bonzo
e. Fluffy
f. Wago
g. Babsy
h. Hokie
i. Sophie
j. Sluggo

Gary Burghoff as Radar

37. REGULAR ARMY

This quiz has to do with regulations, rules, and military terminology. See if you can fit into the military life.

1. If Henry Blake signed a form instead of initialing it, what would he have to do?

2. B.J. once said the army is like the AMA. Why?

3. Every army-issued pair of pants has a code 764J tag on it. What does the tag say?

4. What is a 04WW NUG?

5. Where was the 4077 located, exactly? (Korea is not the right answer.)

6. What were the markings on the bomb that landed in the compound?

7. What does ACFIN mean?

8. What was the official form Radar had to fill out when he went home?

9. What camp did the Potters have a house in?

10. How did Potter make Klinger's reenlistment oath unofficial?

38. RANK MATCHING

Match the rank with the character's name.

1. Sergeant
2. Captain
3. Major General
4. Private
5. General
6. Lieutenant Colonel
7. Colonel
8. Lieutenant
9. Brigadier General
10. Corporal

a. Korshak
b. Nurse Kellye
c. Wendell Peterson
d. Sparky
e. Roy Dupree
f. Clayton
g. Addison Collins
h. Alvin Houlihan
i. Tony Baker
j. Donald Penobscott

39. THE M∗A∗S∗H-OHOLICS MINDBOGGLERS

These are the toughest of the tough. If you consider yourself a M*A*S*H-OHOLIC you should have no problem with these next ten questions.

1. Hawkeye wanted to get in touch with Marilyn Monroe. So he called a certain company in the States, spoke to a receptionist named Madge, and said he was Ted Williams. What company did Madge work for?

2. What was Charles's home phone number?

3. Who was Mr. Buttinsky?

4. What was Hawkeye's first guess at what B.J. stands for?

5. What was Capt. Spaulding's first name?

6. Four actors—Harry Morgan, Charles Aidman, Dennis Dugan, and John Orchard—appeared in the show as two different characters. Can you name the pair of characters played by each of the four actors?

7. What was the name of the company from whom Hawkeye and Trapper got their gorilla outfits?

8. Gen. MacArthur was supposed to come to the 4077. What was his estimated time of arrival?

9. What did Maj. Carter, Maj. Brooks and Ens. Troy have in common?

10. What was the Rainbow Bridge?

40. LET'S GO TO THE MOVIES

This quiz has to do with the movies that were shown at the camp. See if you can recall any of these footage follies.

1. In the Movietone News film, what was the person's name who delivered the pitch on giving blood?

2. What do the movies *Clean As a Whistle, Hansel and Regretel,* and *Buy You a Drink, Sailor?* have in common?

3. What was the name of the movie Frank narrated?

4. Hawkeye wanted to get the movie *The Moon Is Blue* so badly that he went to the film supplier's office and changed its label with another film. What was that other movie?

5. Potter said, "There are three things that make a good movie." What were those three things?

6. What was the address of the Tabasco Film Company, Henry's favorite film supplier?

7. What was Potter's all-time favorite movie?

8. Radar traded the movie *Gilda*, starring Rita Hayworth, to Sparky only to find out that wasn't the movie in the film case. What was the movie he gave away?

9. During the World Series highlights movie, Charles sliced the screen up with a knife. Why?

10. What was the name of the Sonja Henie hygiene film?

41. WHERE DID THEY COME FROM?

Each one of these people showed up at the 4077 at one time or another. What TV show did they come from? Match the actor or actress to his/her original show.

1. John Ritter
2. Linda Kelsey
3. Gregory Harrison
4. Joan Van Ark
5. Larry Wilcox
6. Robert Ito
7. Bart Braverman
8. Ron Howard
9. Stuart Margolin
10. Edward Winter

a. *Happy Days*
b. *Soap*
c. *Three's Company*
d. *Vega$*
e. *Lou Grant*
f. *The Rockford Files*
g. *Knots Landing*
h. *Trapper John, M.D.*
i. *Quincy, M.E.*
j. *CHiPs*

42. MAIL CALL

1. From where did Klinger, Hawkeye, and B.J. order their blue winter coats with fur collars?

2. What "fine leather" did Donald Penobscott send Margaret?

3. Why was Hawkeye's mail sent to someone else?

4. Why was Henry sent a shoebox with bank statements and check stubs in it?

5. What did Radar do so that he would get mail?

6. After B.J. and Hawkeye saved a Greek soldier's life, what did the boy's father send them?

7. Trapper received a letter in the mail from his daughters. There was also a box with the letter. What was in the box?

8. All the people at the 4077 received letters from grade-school kids. What grade were the kids in?

9. Who received the mystery in the mail and let the whole camp read it?

10. What did Charles have his parents send him to help ward off the cold?

43. WHAT DID THEY SAY?

This is just another example of the wit and wisdom of the 4077 staff. Recall the sayings? Just fill in the blanks.

1. Hawkeye: "Give me an _____ or give me death."

2. Referring to Hawkeye, Potter said: "He's witty, suave, and leans toward _____."

3. Hawkeye to Frank: "Frank, the only way you'll get killed is if you _____."

4. Henry, referring to his desk: ". . . cut off a man's legs and steal his _____."

5. Hawkeye: "I'll love you in war and peace or _____ or any of the classics."

6. Said by Radar to Potter on Potter's way back from having a boil lanced: "How'd the boil go, _____?"

7. Henry: "If it weren't for the _____ we'd be having a good time."

8. Margaret to Frank: "I'll be the _____ your wife won't understand."

9. Radar's parents told him: "The _____ is the devil's slipcover."

10. Trapper: "I never met a nurse that didn't _____."

11. Radar: "Last call for coffee before it _____."

12. Father Mulcahy:" _____, the Lord moves in mysterious ways, but you take the cake."

44. WHICH DOESN'T BELONG?

Of the three choices for each question, one of the answers does not belong. Try to eliminate the wrong answers.

1. What famous character did Klinger *never* dress as?
   (a) Bess Truman   (b) The Statue of Liberty
   (c) Lady Godiva

2. Though Hawkeye seemed to be antiarmy, he took on some military duties. Which one had Hawkeye *never* been?
   (a) CO   (b) ROK   (c) OD

3. Which was *not* a chopper pilot's name?
   (a) O'Brien   (b) Compton   (c) Hodges

4. Which is *not* a radio operator Radar has talked to?
   (a) Sparky   (b) Lumpy   (c) Dusty

5. Which of these bad weather conditions *never* hit the 4077?
   (a) hailstorm   (b) windstorm   (c) heatwave

6. Which of these side jobs has Klinger *never* done at the 4077?
   (a) mechanic   (b) cook   (c) bartender

7. Hawkeye always gave Radar a good ribbing. What did Hawkeye *never* tease Radar about?
   (a) his height   (b) his baldness   (c) his youth

8. Many times the people at the 4077 were on an assignment away from camp. Sometimes they didn't make it back right away. Of these choices, which pair was *never* stranded together?
   (a) Hawkeye and Margaret   (b) B.J. and Radar
   (c) Klinger and Charles

9. Radar broke out in a rash easily. Which did *not* make him break out?
   (a) seeing a woman   (b) chop suey   (c) becoming a corporal

10. Frank was put in charge of the "bug out." Which of these items did he *not* allow to leave the camp?
   (a) Radar's critters   (b) the dart board   (c) the still

45. VIOLENCE

Although this show took place during a war, very few violent acts were committed. Sure, there were a few, but can you remember all the details?

1. Frank and Klinger got in a fight and wrestled around the OR. Why?

2. Trapper had to box a marine so Nurse Cutler would be able to stay at the 4077. What was Trapper's fighting name on the back of his robe?

3. Hawkeye punched Frank and was put under house arrest. Why was he finally cleared of all charges?

4. Why did Cowboy, the chopper pilot, try to kill Henry Blake?

5. Who was the soldier Father Mulcahy punched?

6. A Korean soldier jumped off an operating table, attacked an orderly with a scalpel, and cut a nurse's arm. Then Klinger entered. What happened next?

7. Frank was in the shower when a soldier entered who wanted to hold Frank hostage because he wouldn't let him go home. What actor played the soldier?

8. The 4077 was under sniper attack for some time. Finally a chopper put a stop to it with machine gun fire. Later the reason for the attack was determined. What was it?

9. After fighting, on and off, for a long time, a regulation boxing match was set up between Klinger and Zale. Who was the only person to get hit?

10. How did Charles get his tooth broken?

46. A NAME IS A NAME IS A NAME

Many of the staff at the 4077 have special names for each other. They may not be nicknames; I call them pet names. Can you recall them?

1. What did Potter call Father Mulcahy?
2. What did Hawkeye call B.J.?
3. What did Charles call Hawkeye?
4. What did Potter call Radar?
5. What did Radar call Hawkeye and B.J.?
6. What did B.J. call Hawkeye?
7. What did Trapper call Margaret?
8. What did Hawkeye call Henry?
9. What did Radar call Potter?
10. What did Frank call Margaret?
11. What did Klinger's ex-wife call Klinger?
12. What did Hawkeye call Trapper John?
13. What did Charles call all doctors?
14. What did Potter call Mrs. Potter?
15. What did Radar call Margaret?
16. What did Frank call all Koreans?
17. What did Gen. Hamilton call Potter?
18. What did Hawkeye call his father.
19. What did Hawkeye's father call him?
20. What did Frank call Radar?

47. M*A*S*H-RABILIA

Many tokens of appreciation were given at the 4077. This quiz is based on those gifts and novelties.

1. When Park Sung, the Korean agricultural student, went to the States to work for Radar, the camp gave him a party and three going-away presents. What were they?

2. Blake was going to give a present to a nurse friend, but it and other things were stolen. Hawkeye discovered that Ho-John had taken them. What was the gift Henry wanted to give the nurse?

3. What did Radar leave Hawkeye?

4. Charles spent a lot of money on what he thought was a valuable piece of Korean artwork. Later he found out it was worthless junk. What was this item?

5. What little trinket did Radar's mother send him?

6. What gift did Klinger give a Lebanese soldier whose face was burned?

7. Hawkeye needed a pair of boots. After some wheeling and dealing to get them, he had to give Frank a surprise birthday party to fill his part of the bargain. On this birthday of Frank's, what did Margaret give him?

8. Hawkeye and Trapper replaced a vase Frank was sending to his wife with something else. What was that other item?

9. The day Henry left, what did he give Radar?

10. At Potter's mortgage-burning party, what did the gang give the colonel?

48. TRUE OR FALSE

1. Klinger was a pool hustler as a kid.

2. Donald and Margaret's wedding cake was banana-flavored.

3. When Dr. Inga Halverson left the 4077, she was transferred to another MASH unit.

4. Father Mulcahy wrote a war song.

5. Potter had a bright yellow bathrobe.

6. Charles had a younger brother.

7. The latrine blew up on Henry twice.

8. Before being sent to Korea, Frank was chief surgeon at Fort Wayne General Hospital.

9. Henry did not have a son.

10. The same actor played Donald Penobscott every time he appeared at the 4077.

49. WHO WAS THAT PERSON?

Many of the characters referred to people back home. We never see them, but the names just seem to stick in our minds. Match the person's name to the description of how we might remember him/her.

1. Floyd Hayden

   a. Charles's favorite recording artist

2. Mary Jo Carpenter

   b. Henry Blake's next-door neighbor

3. Mr. Witz

   c. Klinger's best friend

4. Monty the Butcher

   d. one of Radar's pen pals

5. Enrico Caruso

   e. the inventor of the magic suction machine

6. Gus Nagie

   f. B.J.'s father-in-law

7. Dagwood the Cat

   g. Klinger's ex-wife's boyfriend

8. Dr. Wanginstein

   h. Radar's neighbor

9. Doc Schumacher

   i. played Ping-Pong in a movie

10. Milt Jaffee

   j. lived across the street from Potter

50. GENERALLY SPEAKING

Many generals found their way into the 4077's camp. This next set of questions has to do with those famous generals.

1. What was Gen. Clayton's first name?

2. What was Gen. Hamilton's son's name?

3. What was Gen. Nat Morrison's wife's name?

4. A general's son was wounded. In order to be near him, the general moved his whole operation to the 4077. Shortly after, his son died. What was the general's name?

5. Gen. Korshak wanted Hawkeye for his private doctor. What did Korshak always say about Hawkeye and his sense of humor?

6. Where did Margaret first serve under Gen. Bradley Barker?

7. What did Gen. Mitchell give the 4077?

8. What did Gen. Steele and his three brothers have in common?

9. Where did Gen. Kelly die?

10. Why did Gen. Hamilton owe Potter a favor?

51. LOCAL INDIGENOUS PERSONNEL (LIP)

Match the LIPs with the description of how you remember them.

1. Dr. Pak

2. Cho Man Chin

3. Cho Lin

4. Kim Luck

5. Mai Ping

6. Sam Pack

7. Park Sung

8. Mr. Quang

9. Kyong Soon

10. Syn Paik

a. a name used by five Koreans to get medical help.

b. an ROK officer

c. Mulligan's girl; he asked Radar to look after her

d. the first bartender at the officers' club

e. a Korean salesman

f. set up marriages between American soldiers and Korean call girls

g. the Korean woman Hawkeye fell in love with

h. the North Korean surgeon Hawkeye and B.J. tried to pass off as South Korean

i. the Korean student who went to the States to help Radar

j. the Ping-Pong champ who was engaged to Soony

(Right) Loretta Swit as "Hot Lips" Houlihan in "Dreams" (1979)

52. "DREAMS"

This test is based on the episode "Dreams."

1. What color was the tie B.J. wore in his dream?
2. What was Potter doing in his dream?
3. What did Klinger see in the window of Tony Paco's?
4. How did Charles try to save his patient in his dream?
5. Which arm did Hawkeye have to give up first?
6. Where did Potter fall asleep when he had his dream?
7. What was Father Mulcahy's dream about?
8. What was Margaret wearing in her dream?
9. What was the name of the newspaper Klinger was reading in the dream?
10. Klinger's dream was to return to Toledo. How did he get there?

53. IN LIVING COLOR

Can you remember the colors of things? Some people have no trouble at all remembering colors, others have a rough time. See if you can recall colors, and for those of you with black-and-white TVs the answers will be in your shade too.

1. What color was Trapper's robe?

2. What was B.J.'s favorite color?

3. What color were the flags and license plates on Gen. Clayton's jeep?

4. What was the color of the beer bottle labels?

5. Hawkeye's favorite color was what?

6. What color were the credits?

7. What color was Spearchucker's hat?

8. What color were B.J.'s tennis shoes?

9. What color would Klinger never wear because it matched his skin?

10. What was the color of Klinger's puffy slippers?

54. FEMALE GUEST STARS

Match the character with the actress who played the role.

1. Lt. Erika Johnson
2. Miki Baker
3. Aggie O'Shea
4. Peg Hunnicut
5. Col. Reese
6. Inga Halverson
7. Lt. Louise Simmons
8. Carlye
9. Lt. Edwina ("Eddie") Ferguson

a. Blythe Danner
b. Mary Kay Place
c. Arlene Golonka
d. Joan Van Ark
e. Susan Saint James
f. Linda Kelsey
g. Catherine Bergstrom
h. Mariette Hartley
i. Mary Wickes

55. M*A*S*H-AMATICS

This test deals with numbers. Heights, weights, sizes, and miscella-
neous statistics are included in this teaser. This may be hard for
some, but just simple addition for others.

1. What was the combination to the company safe?

2. How far was it from the 4077 to Seoul?

3. What was B.J.'s shoe size?

4. How old was B.J. when he was drafted?

5. How much did Trapper weigh?

6. How tall was Radar?

7. What was the patient survival rate at the 4077?

8. How much did Klinger pay for a box of cigars?

9. What was the date Col. Potter came to the 4077?

10. What was Klinger's house number in Toledo?

56. SING ME A SONG

There were many songs sung throughout the course of the show, but can you remember which songs and when they were sung? Match the lyrics of the songs to the scenes in which they occurred.

1. Klinger was cutting Potter's hair . . .

    a. "Stormy Weather . . ."

2. Potter in the shower, Father Mulcahy walks in . . .

    b. "We're having a heatwave, a tropical heatwave . . ."

3. Radar paging through the file cabinet . . .

    c. "You oughta be in pictures, wa wa . . ."

4. Hawkeye in the shower the day Inga was coming . . .

    d. "I'll be loving you-ou-ou-ou, ou-ou-ou . . ."

5. Radar testing the PA system . . .

    e. "I love to go swimmin' with bow-legged women . . ."

6. Hawkeye leading the singing on a cold winter night . . .

    f. "A, B, C, D, E, F, G, . . ."

7. Charles and Klinger lost women, got drunk, and sang . . .

    g. "I got a gal in Kalamazoo, zoo, zoo . . ."

8. Hawkeye riding a bike through camp . . .

    h. "Puttin' on the ritz . . ."

9. Klinger was depressed. Potter gave him his discharge. Klinger jumped up and sang . . .

    i. "A pretty girl, RATATATA, is like a melody, RATATATA . . ."

10. Hawkeye singing about Flagg undercover as a chorus girl in Las Vegas . . .

    j. "Daisy, Daisy . . ."

57. ENLISTED PERSONNEL

1. What was Rizzo in charge of?
2. Who was the supply officer?
3. What was Zale's first name?
4. How much did a private earn per month?
5. What was Cowboy's chopper pilot code name?
6. Who were the contestants for the soldier-of-the-month contest?
7. What was Rizzo's first name?
8. What does Igor want to do when he gets home?
9. Which enlisted man had the best knowledge of the roads?
10. Who was Nick Saunders?

58. MALE GUEST STARS

Hint: One of the actors played two different roles.

1. Col. Maurice Hollister	a. Ed Flanders
2. Col. Brighton	b. Ron Howard
3. Cpl. Tony Baker	c. Stuart Margolin
4. Tommy Gillis	d. Jack Riley
5. Capt. Tom Greenly	e. James Stephens
6. Capt. Roy Dupree	f. Ned Beatty
7. Col. Alvin Houlihan	g. Gregory Harrison
8. Pvt. Wendell Peterson	h. Pat Morita
9. Capt. Caplin	i. Andrew Duggan
10. Capt. Spaulding	j. Loudon Wainwright III
11. Capt. Philip Sherman	k. George Lindsey
12. Pvt. David Sheridan	l. John Matuzak
13. Sam Pak	m. Oliver Parker
14. Pvt. Carter	n. James Callahan
15. Capt. Ben Pierce	o. Leslie Nielsen
16. Cpl. Hitalski	p. John Ritter
17. Pvt. George Weston	q. Richard Ely
18. Lt. D.W. Bricker	r. Greg Mullavey
19. Stanley Robbins	

59. TRADING POWER

To get what they wanted, sometimes these crazy MASHers had to do some wheeling and dealing. Can you recall these swapping situations?

1. When the 4077 had to bug out, they needed an old school building and had to trade something with the occupants, ladies of the evening. What did they give these ladies for the building?

2. The day Radar left, what did Klinger trade to get a generator?

3. What movie did Radar trade to Sparky so he would put a phone call through to B.J.'s father-in-law in Oklahoma?

4. Hawkeye was assigned the duty as mess officer. He discovered that 50 meal trays were missing. What did he want to trade to the MASH 8063 for the 50 trays?

5. Radar gave Hawkeye's long underwear to the cook. What did Radar get out of the deal?

6. What did Klinger have to trade to get the book *I, the Jury*?

7. Which of Henry's belongings did Radar trade for the incubator?

8. Margaret made a trade with Charles. He had to train the nurses in a new technique. What did Margaret have to do in return?

9. Frank wouldn't order tomato juice so Radar could surprise Col. Potter. What did Radar have to get from Klinger to give to Frank so he would order the juice?

10. And what did Klinger get out of this deal?

60. MAJ. SIDNEY FREEDMAN

1. Who played Sidney?

2. The first time Sidney came to the 4077 he was going to give Klinger a discharge. For what reason?

3. Sidney suffered a superficial head wound. How did it happen?

4. What did Sidney prescribe for the whole camp to release the pressure?

5. Who did Sidney like to send letters to?

6. What was Sidney's middle name?

7. Where did he like to spend his vacation?

8. In the last episode, Sidney was treating Hawkeye. What one word was he trying to make Hawkeye remember?

9. What did Sidney throw into the camp bonfire?

10. What did Sidney say as he left the 4077 for the last time?

Margaret "Hot Lips" Houlihan and Frank Burns in "Five O'Clock Charlie" (1973)

61. "FIVE O'CLOCK CHARLIE"

1. Where did Charlie get his name? Why did they call him that?
2. How many weeks in a row did Charlie come through?
3. What was Charlie trying to do?
4. The winning bet was 75½ yards. Who won?
5. Who held the bets?
6. Frank wanted to blow Charlie out of the sky. What happened that enabled the 4077 to get the gun?
7. Trapper, Hawkeye, and Radar came to visit Frank and his platoon. How was Trapper dressed?
8. In mocking Frank, Hawkeye was to "count off." What did he say when Radar asked, "Are you one?"
9. How did Trapper and Hawkeye try to help Charlie?
10. What was the final outcome of the show? What happened to the gun, Charlie, and the ammo dump?

62. WHO SAID THAT!

Fill in the blanks with the proper words. Remember, the writers of this show are very clever, so let your imaginations work. It's not as hard as it looks.

1. Hawkeye: "_____ is just a state of mind."

2. Frank: "It was a great _____ till you guys showed up."

3. B.J., while Frank was reading: "What's so absorbing, _____?"

4. Klinger: "To get a beautiful rose, sometimes you have to shovel a lot of _____."

5. Frank: "It's just in your head. But don't think it's _____."

6. Flagg: "All _____ understand everything you say."

7. Hawkeye to Radar: "When this is all over, I'm going to _____ you."

8. B.J. to Charles: "Breaking a _____ is seven years' bad luck."

9. Frank: "_____ don't grow on trees, soldier."

10. Hawkeye: "If it wasn't for Radar, 4077 would just be a _____."

63. HAWKEYE

1. What was the only thing Hawkeye said he brought from home?
2. What kind of job did he have when he was preparing for medical school?
3. When Hawkeye was crowned as chief surgeon, what was used as his scepter?
4. Who was the first patient he cried over?
5. How did he heat his bed?
6. What did he like to do every Thursday?
7. What did he always do to his food before he ate?
8. Koreans were being trained to help in OR and they had to learn English. What did Hawkeye teach them to say?
9. Where did he get his nickname?
10. What was Hawkeye always willing to help Margaret with?

Alan Alda as Hawkeye

64. OOPS! WRONG SHOW

Some of the actors and actresses who played characters on *M*A*S*H* also appeared in other television shows. Match their *M*A*S*H* characters to the other characters they played. This one's not easy.

1. Pvt. Wendell Peterson
2. Capt. Tom Greenly
3. Lt. Erika Johnson
4. Capt. Roy Dupree
5. Nurse Cutler
6. Tony Baker
7. Lt. Miki Baker
8. Aggie O'Shea
9. Lt. Edwina ("Eddie") Ferguson
10. Capt. Philip Sherman

a. Goober Pyle
b. Gonzo Gates
c. Billie Newman
d. Millie Swanson
e. Sally McMillan
f. Val Ewing
g. Julie Kotter
h. Tom Hartman
i. Angel Martin
j. Richie Cunningham

65. TRAPPER

1. What did Trapper's parents want him to be?

2. What magazine did Trapper read?

3. What was the name of Trapper's winning gurney-derby team?

4. What number was on Trapper's basketball jersey?

5. Trapper's patient, Condon, didn't want to get the "wrong color" blood. What did Trapper do to fix him?

6. Why did Trapper get drunk and try to go AWOL?

7. Hawkeye just missed Trapper when he left. How close in time was this miss?

8. Trapper and Hawkeye were trying to win a pony in a contest. They had to find all the presidents' faces in a hidden picture puzzle. Who was the first face Trapper found?

9. Vinnie Pratt was an old buddy of Trapper's. What did Vinnie call Trapper?

10. How long, according to Hawkeye, did Trapper and Hawkeye live together?

66. STILL STRICTLY RELATIVE

1. What was Zale's daughter's name?
2. In what city did Potter's daughter and son-in-law live?
3. What did Charles's mother do?
4. Name Trapper's daughters.
5. What was Klinger's ex-wife's full maiden name?
6. Where did Charles's grandmother live?
7. What was Rizzo's child's name?
8. What did Henry's mother and Margaret have in common?
9. What did Potter's Uncle Claude collect?
10. What did Potter's son-in-law do for a living?

67. TEASERS

1. Who was Pvt. Charles Lamb?
2. Back home, what was Frank's receptionist's name?
3. Who was Orville Carver?
4. Radar's code name was Snow White. What was Klinger's code name while he was at the aid station?
5. What was the name of the Crab Apple Cove newspaper?
6. What did Frank use his wife's fruitcake for?
7. Why didn't Frank want Hawkeye to give him a foot check?
8. What phobia did Hawkeye have?
9. What was the first article Aggie O'Shea wrote?

B.J., Radar, and Father Mulcahy in "Radar's Goodbye" (79-80 season)

68. RADAR

1. How old was Radar's dad when Radar was born?

2. Radar was tired of being kidded about being short. He sent away for elevator shoes. What was the name of the company?

3. What did Radar tell Hawkeye and Trapper about Flagg before they met him?

4. What were Radar's earmuffs made of?

5. What did he always wear on a date?

6. Radar had his tonsils taken out. What did Hawkeye and B.J. trade to get him ten gallons of strawberry ice cream and a bottle of twelve-year-old scotch for themselves?

7. What size dress did Radar's mother wear?

8. What was the first thing Radar said to Col. Potter?

9. Radar was selling shoes from the Style-Right Shoe Company of Storm Lake, Iowa. They cost $8.95 and an extra $1.95 for an extra-high instep. What did the shoes look like?

69. HENRY BLAKE

1. According to Henry, what was the first thing he learned in commander school?

2. What was Henry's waist size?

3. Where did Henry meet his wife?

4. What were Mrs. Blake's measurements?

5. How did Blake like his steak?

6. As Henry was getting the chopper to go home, what did he say to Radar?

7. Henry's desk was put through a lot of strain. What were the two things that happened to his desk?

8. What did Mrs. Blake want to do to the furniture before Henry arrived home?

9. What did Henry's parents go to Niagara Falls for?

10. Henry received a letter from his wife. She gave him permission to fool around, but at the same time Henry thought she might be fooling around too. After talking to her on the phone he found out she had a date for the Pumpkin Dance at the Country Club. What was the occupation of the man she was going to the dance with?

McLean Stevenson as Henry Blake

70. ALAN ALDA'S FAVORITE EPISODES

Give brief descriptions of the following shows.

1. "Inga"
2. "Dear Sigmund"
3. "Dear Sis"
4. "Fallen Idol"
5. "In Love and War"
6. "Hepatitis"
7. "War of Nerves"
8. "Comrade in Arms"—part 1
9. "Comrade in Arms"—part 2
10. "The Party"

Margaret and Hawkeye become "Comrades in Arms."

71. COMMON GROUND

Although the people at the 4077 came from different parts of the country, different ways of life, some of them did have something in common. What did the pairs below have in common? The hints will help.

1. Potter and Klinger   *hint*   it's a habit
2. Potter and Gen. Korshak   *hint*   two faces
3. Hawkeye and Blake   *hint*   the eyes have it
4. Trapper and B.J.   *hint*   go west
5. Frank and Trapper   *hint*   it's relative
6. Frank and Henry Blake   *hint*   it takes practice
7. Father Mulcahy and Trapper   *hint*   be a sport
8. Charles and Father Mulcahy   *hint*   it takes heart
9. Hawkeye and Inga Halverson   *hint*   father's shadow
10. Trapper and Radar   *hint*   a pair of hearts

72. FRANK

1. What operation did Frank ask Hawkeye and Trapper to perform on him? They were dressed like gorillas at the time.

2. What was Frank's only pet as a child?

3. What did Henry once say about Frank that Potter totally agreed with?

4. What was the name of the sickness Frank discovered?

5. Why did Frank become a doctor?

6. How did Frank like his pork chops?

7. Where did he hide his bank account number at home?

8. How much did Frank pay for the answers to his medical college finals?

9. What song did Frank play on the spoons?

10. Why was Frank the president of the stamp club in high school?

73. THE TIME CAPSULE

Margaret got the idea of burying a time capsule with something from everyone at the 4077. If the time capsule were to be found, the finder would know all about them. What did each of these people leave for the capsule?

1. Hawkeye
2. Nurse Kellye
3. Rizzo
4. Margaret
5. Potter
6. B.J.
7. Frank
8. Charles
9. Klinger
10. Father Mulcahy

74. MARGARET

1. Margaret received a letter from her husband. Her name was on the envelope but not on the letter inside. What was the name of the woman Donald was writing to?

2. What did Margaret's mother do?

3. What did Hawkeye and B.J. do to Margaret's husband after his stag party?

4. While in charge of camp beautification, what did Margaret have built?

5. What did Frank reveal about himself and Margaret when he thought he was dying?

6. What was the first military record Margaret falsified?

7. Who took out her appendix?

8. What author did Margaret like?

9. Col. Baldwin mistook Margaret for a lady of the evening. What was he wearing the night he attacked her in the VIP tent?

10. Did Margaret have 20/20 vision?

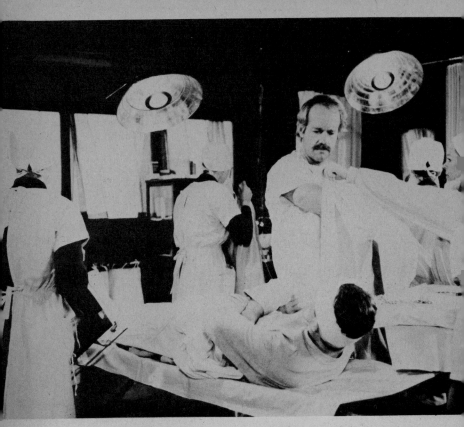

B.J. prepares to operate.

75. DOCTORS

1. Who played Dr. Borelli?

2. What was Spearchucker's medical specialty?

3. How long had Frank been a doctor?

4. Potter and Charles had the mumps. Their replacement, Dr. Newsome, didn't work out. What happened to him?

5. Who was the famous plastic surgeon that came to the 4077 to "fix" a soldier's nose?

6. Who wanted Charles and B.J. to write an article on the operation they performed on Cpl. Howzer?

7. According to Hawkeye, what was Dr. Kline's specialty?

8. A lawyer, Capt. William Bainbridge, was sent to the 4077 instead of a doctor. B.J. and Hawkeye trained him for surgery. Who was the actor who played this lawyer turned doctor?

9. Sidney was not the first psychiatrist to come to the 4077. Who was?

10. The Chinese doctor, Lin Tam, gave the 4077 nine wounded soldiers. Volunteers from the 4077 had to go pick them up. After talking to Dr. Lin Tam, they discovered he went to school in the States. Where?

76. WHAT DOES IT SAY ON . . .

1. . . . the picture Margaret's dad got from MacArthur?
2. . . . the box full of the things Margaret was returning to Frank?
3. . . . Col. Flagg's top-secret telegram?
4. . . . the flyers that were in the CIA's propaganda bomb?
5. . . . Frank's picture of his mother? Hawkeye wrote it.
6. . . . the sign over the 8063?
7. . . . Klinger's bowling shirt?
8. . . . the handgun Margaret mother's got on her wedding night?
9. . . . Radar's going-away cake?

77. KLINGER

1. What brand of cigars did Klinger smoke?

2. What was Max's middle initial?

3. What did Klinger try to do with the jeep with the squeaky seat?

4. What was his Korean wife's name?

5. Klinger's mom didn't know he was in Korea. Where did she think he was?

6. How did Klinger almost get his Section 8? It had nothing to do with dressing as a woman.

7. What was his last wish?

8. Klinger was practicing Potter's signature. What did the colonel say he was doing wrong?

9. According to Klinger, what happened to his mother on the way to the hospital the day he was born?

10. What language did his parents speak?

78. FATHER MULCAHY

1. What did the good Father do before he became a priest?

2. What did Father Mulcahy call his sister, Sister Maria Angelica?

3. Father tried to calm down a Korean soldier, he kept saying, "Bung chow." He thought this meant peace. What did it actually mean?

4. Father once said he wasn't much on baseball, but he was partial to one team. What was the team?

5. How was Father Mulcahy dressed for his special sermon with Cardinal Reardon?

6. Who were the Father's childhood idols?

7. Father Mulcahy had a T-shirt from Florida. What city in Florida was written on the front of the shirt?

8. What letter was on Father Mulcahy's baseball cap?

9. At age twelve, Father played spin-the-bottle and always got to kiss Patricia Duggan. What did he come to know about her?

10. Father's sister, the Benedictine nun, was an athelete. What sport was she involved in?

79. A TOUCH OF COLOR

Fill in the blanks with the correct colors.

1. B.J.'s long underwear was _____.

2. Hawkeye and Carlye had an apartment in Boston. They painted it _____.

3. Hawkeye: "_____ olives for martinis are from the_____ market of _____ China."

4. Trapper's basketball jersey had _____ with _____ trim.

5. Gen. Clayton to Hawkeye: "You don't want to give the _____, _____, and _____ a _____ eye, do you?"

6. B.J. painted his motorcycle _____.

7. On Radar's going-away cake it said Good-bye Radar in _____ frosting.

8. Frank: ". . . fighting the _____ stain, communism, makes me see _____."

9. The shirt Hawkeye was wearing in the introduction of every show was _____.

10. Father Mulcahy's hat was _____.

80. B.J.

1. Who bought B.J. his first drink in Korea?

2. What was the name of his racing cockroach?

3. B.J.'s wife, Peg, took a job at a restaurant to make extra money. What was the job?

4. Who put B.J. through medical school?

5. What was the medical school he went to?

6. B.J. told one of his patients, Cpl. Marsh, to break a leg. What was so unusual about that?

7. What did "bodabebaba" mean to B.J.?

8. B.J. was injured. He had a compartment hemorrhage. Where was this injury?

9. B.J.'s military training only lasted five weeks. Where was the training?

10. B.J. was awarded a medal for his act of bravery while under fire, but he turned it down. What was the medal?

81. PROMOTIONS

1. How many regulars on the show were promoted?

2. The day B.J. arrived, Hawkeye promoted Radar so he could get into the officers' club. What rank did Hawkeye bestow on Radar?

3. How many promotions did chopper pilot Toby Hill receive in six months?

4. How did Hawkeye get Radar promoted to second lieutenant?

5. How many times was Father Mulcahy's name submitted for a promotion?

6. Who said, "How could a short, near-sighted, lower-class clerk become a lieutenant? Impossible."?

7. What was the name of the soldier who threatened Charles that if he wasn't promoted to sergeant, it would be Charles's fault and he would get even.

8. Who was on the promotion board when Klinger became a sergeant?

9. When Father Mulcahy was passed over for promotion he wanted to prove he was worthy of advancement. He went to the aid station to bring a wounded boy back. What happened on the way back to camp?

10. Who pinned the good Father with his captain bars when he did get promoted?

82. POTTER

1. What kind of mattress did Potter have on his bunk?

2. Where did the colonel serve his residency?

3. Who was Potter's favorite singer?

4. The Potters' anniversary was on the second of February. Why did Sherman pick that day?

5. Where did the colonel meet his wife for their second honeymoon?

6. What was Potter's favorite comic strip?

7. What kind of camera did Potter have?

8. What did Potter forget to do on his thirty-fifth anniversary?

9. What was Potter's religion?

10. What did the name Puddin' Head mean to Potter?

83. M*A*S*H-AMATICS PLUS

Here's another test of numbers. I hope it adds up for you.

1. How much did Hawkeye figure he got paid for each operation?

2. How tall was B.J.'s wife?

3. How many MASH units were in Korea?

4. What was the population of Hawkeye's hometown?

5. How much money did Charles win from Col. Baldwin? He was the colonel who sent Charles to the 4077.

6. What was Hawkeye's shoe size?

7. How far was it from the 4077 to Tokyo?

8. According to Klinger, what size pants did Charles wear?

9. How many people did the 4077 try to fit into a jeep to break a world record?

10. How far was it from the 4077 to the front line?

84. CHARLES

1. Where was Charles stationed before he was transferred to the 4077?

2. How did Charles send letters to his parents?

3. When Charles refused to quit playing his French horn, what did B.J. and Hawkeye refuse to do?

4. What was the name of Charles's polo pony?

5. As a teen, Charles was in love with a Swedish girl named Christina. Where did he know her from?

6. Why did Charles suddenly start to snore?

7. While on his way to Tokyo, Charles was stranded with Klinger. They came across wounded soldiers. He had to use some of his expensive clothing for bandages. What were those bits of garment?

8. Why did Charles take over Klinger's job as company clerk?

9. Charles was the only one who could get newspapers in camp. His sister sent them to him, first class. The May fifth issue was missing. Charles accused everyone of stealing it. What happened to the paper?

10. Charles put a lot of money on the World Series between the Giants and the Dodgers. Which team did he pick to win?

85. MORE NICKNAMES

1. Freddie Nichols
2. Lt. Mitchell
3. Dr. Myron Herzog
4. Gen. Rivers
5. Gen. Torgensen
6. Dr. Norman Chase
7. Klinger's father
8. Lt. Col. Lacy
9. Mr. Wang
10. Sgt. Parker

a. Squint
b. Butch
c. Whiplash
d. Killer
e. The Ice Man
f. Bud
g. Torgy
h. Fast
i. Smilin' Jack
j. Ol' Yellow Teeth

86. CARDS, ANYONE?

1. Who taught Father Mulcahy to play cards?

2. What kind of hand did Frank have the first time he won a poker game?

3. Hawkeye called him the greatest poker face and said that if he kept it up he would end up on Mt. Rushmore. Who was Hawkeye talking about?

4. After losing some money, Father Mulcahy decided to quit and curl up with a book. What was the book?

5. Charles professed to be a bridge expert, but he never won the 4077 bridge tournament. Who played in this championship?

6. Charles kept winning at strip poker. It was bad enough to lose to Charles, but what else did the crew have going against them?

7. Charles lost $200 to B.J. at poker. Suddenly Charles was on a winning streak. But Radar found a flaw in his winning. What did Radar detect Charles do when he was bluffing?

8. Hawkeye was trying to cheat Sgt. Baker at poker. Radar was on the other side of camp with a telescope calling Baker's cards to Hawkeye by radio. Then something blocked Radar's sight. What was that something?

9. What kind of gun did Hawkeye win in a poker game?

10. There was a foursome in bridge that attracted Col. Flagg's interest. Potter and Hawkeye were two of the players, the other two were Korean. Who were they?

87. DOUBLE TROUBLE (2)

All these questions have two answers.

1. What was the name and phone number of Frank's stock-broker?

2. What movie star did Charles once have dinner with and how did he prove it?

3. Potter painted Hawkeye's picture twice. What were the two poses?

4. Radar met a nurse named Patty. Her hometown was not far from Radar's hometown. Where was she from and how far from Radar's hometown was it?

5. Klinger's camp paper had a beauty column. What was the name of the column and who wrote it?

6. Frank was snooping at a letter Hawkeye planted. The letter was regarding a hot tip on the stockmarket. Who was the letter to and what was the name of the company Hawkeye referred to?

7. Aggie O'Shea promised she would send everyone something from Tokyo. She sent Hawkeye a twelve-year-old bottle of scotch and Margaret perfumed soap. What did she send B.J. and Charles?

8. Potter said he was a POW during World War I. He got stranded somewhere and was taken prisoner. How long was he stranded and where was he?

9. Hawkeye and Trapper called Chicago to order barbecued ribs. What was the name of the rib restaurant and what did they forget to order?

10. While on R&R, Frank attacked a general and his wife in a bathhouse. What happened to Frank after this?

88. HAWKEYE PIERCE

1. What magazine did Hawkeye subscribe to?

2. According to Hawkeye, who was the greatest man that ever lived?

3. When Hawkeye called to order ribs from Chicago he said he was Crampton Lamont. What did Mr. Lamont do for a living?

4. How did Hawkeye break the ice with Potter when the colonel first arrived?

5. Hawkeye was injured the day Radar left. What happened?

6. After Frank's lecture and three days without sleep, Hawkeye said he knew what the Chinese wanted from America. What was it?

7. B.J. pulled off the best practical joke. How did Hawkeye get back at him?

8. Hawkeye was pay officer. He was $10 over his allotment of cash. What did he do with it?

9. During the first cease-fire, Hawkeye ended relationships with three nurses. How did he do that?

10. What article of clothing did Hawkeye put on that he thought would make Margaret respond?

89. STILL SINGIN' A SONG

Match the situation with the song being sung.

1. For his floor show at Rosie's, Klinger sang . . .

2. The camp was watching a movie. The film broke, and they all started to sing . . .

3. As the stripper in the USO show did her act, she sang . . .

4. Trapper in the OR . . .

5. Father Mulcahy at the piano, everyone joined in . . .

6. Hawkeye in the bathtub . . .

7. Klinger working at his sewing machine . . .

8. The morning after Hawkeye went on the wagon . . .

9. Hawkeye made a bet with B.J. The loser had to stand on a mess table and sing . . .

10. The MASH crew built a huge bonfire. As they watched it burn they sang . . .

a. "Keep the home fires burning . . ."

b. "Cuddle up a little closer . . ."

c. "That's why the lady is a tramp . . ."

d. "I was dancin' with my darlin' to the Tennessee Waltz . . ."

e. "You'll never know just how much I love you . . ."

f. "I've got you under my skin . . ."

g. "There's a bright golden haze on Korea . . ."

h. "Anchors away, my boy. Anchors away . . ."

i. "Gee, mom, I want to go home . . ."

j. "You're the top, you're the tower of Pisa . . ."

90. ROSIE'S

1. What did it say on the front window of Rosie's bar?

2. Who was Rosie's booze supplier?

3. What did Charles wear when he tended bar at Rosie's?

4. What was the name of the hot rice dish served there?

5. Rosie kicked a dog out of her bar for being a lush. What was the dog's name?

6. How much did a bottle of grape Nehi cost at Rosie's?

7. How much did Hawkeye pay to rent the shack behind Rosie's bar?

8. After getting her ribs broken in a bar fight, Rosie had to let the 4077 officers run her place. She gave them three orders. One was to be nice to her supply officer, another was to collect 30 percent of all tips from every waitress. What was the last instruction?

9. Trying to escape the war, Hawkeye and B.J. went to Rosie's. What did they want to do so they wouldn't have to go back?

10. Who drank grape Nehi after Radar went home?

Hawkeye, Radar, and B.J. in Rosie's bar

91. THE SPORTS PAGE—PAGE TWO

1. What camp record did Potter hold?

2. What was the name of Hawkeye's entry in the gurney derby?

3. Who was the only person, according to Potter, who could beat him at horseshoes?

4. Where was the basketball hoop?

5. What MASH record did Klinger break?

6. What did Hawkeye and B.J. use for checkers?

7. What medical equipment did Hawkeye and Trapper use for a Ping-Pong table and net?

8. What was the bet B.J. and Hawkeye made before the MASH Olympics?

9. What were the two toys Klinger invented?

10. Aside from being a marine, Sgt. Ubanchek was a pro at a particular sport. What was his claim to fame?

92. TRUE OR FALSE

1. Hawkeye was the best man for Margaret's wedding.
2. Hawkeye bought the garbage Frank auctioned off.
3. Frank shot B.J.
4. Father Mulcahy was a bartender at the officers' club.
5. Hawkeye once helped Radar's mother deliver a baby cow over the phone.
6. Potter once had a mustache.
7. Klinger had two brothers.
8. Frank's wife found out about Frank and Margaret.
9. Potter had a fling with another woman.
10. Father Mulcahy had two sisters who were both nuns.

93. STUMPERS

Again, I propose the tough ones. Only a real M*A*S*H-OHOLIC will be able to answer the next ten questions.

1. Who was "the Barracuda"?

2. In the office file cabinet, under what were the mine field maps filed?

3. In the "Dreams" episode, what was the address of Tony Paco's?

4. What did Hawkeye and B.J. order from Abercrombie and Fitch?

5. What was the 8063's chaplain's name?

6. What is the time difference between Korea and the States?

7. The last word on a crossword puzzle was number 38 across. Five letters. A Yiddish word meaning bedbug. What was the word?

8. There was a two-city relay to get a phone call from the 4077 to any city in the States. What was the relay combination?

9. What was the motto of the Style-Right Shoe Company of Storm Lake, Iowa?

10. What were the circumstances of Potter's speeding ticket? How fast was he going? And what was the posted speed?

94. HAWKEYE'S ARMY

Hawkeye had his own way with the military. He had his own sayings and he did whatever he wanted. He even said whatever he wanted to whomever he wanted. Remember Hawkeye's army?

1. Everyone else went on R&R, but according to Hawkeye, R&R for Father Mulcahy meant something other than rest and relaxation. What did it mean for the good Father?

2. Flagg said he was with the CIA. What did Hawkeye say it stood for?

3. Hawkeye's serial number was 3. Why?

4. Hawkeye built a tower out of tongue depressors. Each depressor represented a boy that came through the 4077. What did Hawkeye call this monument?

5. In referring to Frank, M.D. meant something other than medical doctor. What did it mean?

6. Gen. Korshak was told by Hawkeye he had to take care of himself. He did need a personal physician, and he had to slow down or he would kill himself. Korshak said he could take an order. What was Hawkeye's response?

7. Why did Hawkeye go to Panmunjon?

8. Gen. Steele brought Hawkeye up on charges. What were the counts?

9. What was Hawkeye's first order as commanding officer?

10. According to Hawkeye, what did OD stand for?

95. AWARDS

Since the 4077 first made its appearance on the TV screen, the cast, directors, and writers have won many awards, not to mention numerous nominations. This test has to do with those awards.

1. How many Emmys was the show nominated for over the eleven years?

2. In 1977 one episode of M*A*S*H received an Emmy for Outstanding Directing in a Comedy Series (Alan Alda), the Directors' Guild Award (Alan Alda), and the Writers' Guild Award (teleplay by Alan Alda). This episode was also nominated for four other awards that same year. What was the title of this episode?

3. Did the TV pilot ever receive an award?

4. Over the last eleven years, how many Emmys has the show won?

5. Did Gary Burghoff ever win an Emmy?

6. In 1975 Alan Alda won the People's Choice Award for Favorite Male Television Performer. Another actor won the award that same year. Who tied Alda for the award?

7. What actor was nominated for the Emmy for Outstanding Performance by an Actor in a Supporting Role in a Comedy every year he was on the show, but never won it?

8. Of the four nominations for actors in the first season, how many won an award?

9. What year did Alan Alda win his first Emmy for the show and what was the award for?

10. What three People's Choice Awards did this show win in 1980?

96. MORE GUEST STARS

Here's a hint: two actors played the same character at two different times. . . .

1. Col. Daniel Webster Tucker
2. Dr. Steve Newsome
3. Gen. Hammon
4. Sgt. Lyle Wesson
5. Scully
6. Cpl. Jarvis
7. Gen. Robert Kelly
8. Lt. Col. Donald Penobscott
9. Condon
10. Bob Wilson

a. Joshua Bryant
b. Anthony Alda
c. James Gregory
d. Miles Watson
e. Beeson Carroll
f. Edward Hermann
g. Alex Karras
h. Dennis Duggan
i. G. Wood
j. Pat Hingle
k. Mike Henry

97. FILL IN THE BLANKS

1. Henry Blake to Gen. Kelly: "I got it all _____ backwards."

2. Potter asked Frank if he ever "bugged out." Frank replied, "No, sir, _____."

3. Charles, the moment he arrived at the 4077: "This is an _____ on the buttocks of life."

4. Frank: "There's a war on; there's no time for _____."

5. Hawkeye to Trapper: "When you said you were six three I didn't think you meant _____."

6. Potter, B.J., and Hawkeye are toasting: Potter: "To Harry Truman"; B.J.: "To Bess Truman"; Hawkeye: "To _____."

7. Hawkeye to the Chinese officer at the Rainbow Bridge: "You're doing a big _____ in the midst of a big _____."

8. Radar's last words as he left the 4077: " _____; let's go."

9. Father Mulcahy as he blessed the new OR floor: "Bless this floor. May it be used _____."

10. Hawkeye: "The only good thing that came out of Henry's mouth was _____."

98. REAL TEASERS

1. What kind of night-light did Frank have as a boy?

2. What visiting colonel referred to Charles's hometown as "bean-town"?

3. According to Radar, how long did it take to get the morning paper?

4. Where were the church services conducted?

5. How many regulars were married on the show?

6. What did PM mean to Potter?

7. What happened to that crazy Gen. Steele after he left the 4077?

8. What did the name Helen Rappaport mean to Frank?

9. How did the boxer Gentleman Joe Cavanaugh die?

10. Was Potter a doctor during World War I?

11. Margaret ordered red yarn from the Sears catalogue. She started to make a pot holder. What did she end up making?

12. What was B.J.'s serial number?

13. What was the Franastan Plan?

14. How long did it take Frank to finish med school?

15. Why did they call Walter O'Reilly Radar?

16. What did the names Prince, Lightning, and Norman mean to Hawkeye and Trapper?

17. Who did B.J. know in Quapaw, Oklahoma?

18. How old was Potter when he served in World War I?

19. What pet name did Henry call his daughter, Janey?

20. What was the name of the series that ran in Hawkeye's nude magazine?

99. WHAT ARE YOU GOING TO DO AFTER THE WAR?

In the last show, all the regulars of the 4077 told what they were going to do when they got home. As Potter said, "What will your lives be like?" Can you recall what each of these people were going to do when they got home or wherever they were going?

1. Margaret

2. Hawkeye

3. Igor

4. Rizzo

5. Klinger

6. Potter

7. Father Mulcahy

8. Nurse Kellye

9. B.J.

10. Charles

Scenes from the final M*A*S*H episode, "Goodbye, Farewell and Amen" (1983)

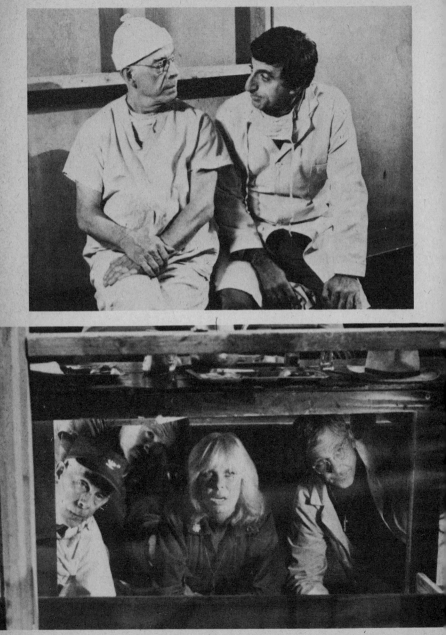

More scenes from "Goodbye, Farewell and Amen"

100. "GOODBYE, FAREWELL, AMEN"

1. Who sponsored the two-and-a-half-hour special?

2. How much did a thirty-second commercial cost advertisers during the airing of the 4077's farewell show?

3. Who was the author of the book Charles gave Margaret?

4. How did Potter know there was a brushfire on its way?

5. How many musicians did Charles work with?

6. Why was the 4077 under enemy fire?

7. Before Margaret made her final decision on where to relocate, she had two other ideas. What were Margaret's first relocation choices?

8. What did Potter tell Klinger about love?

9. What was the last thing Hawkeye said to Father Mulcahy?

10. How did B.J. say good-bye?

101. RIDING OFF INTO THE SUNSET

What type of vehicle took each of these people away from the 4077 for the last time?

1. B.J.
2. Hawkeye
3. Margaret
4. Rizzo
5. Henry
6. Radar
7. Potter
8. Charles
9. Klinger
10. Nurse Kellye

Alan Alda as Hawkeye in "Goodbye, Farewell and Amen"

THE
A*N*S*W*E*R*S

1. The Easy Stuff

1. Alan Alda
2. Wayne Rogers
3. Mike Farrell
4. Larry Linville
5. Harry Morgan
6. McLean Stevenson
7. Gary Burghoff
8. David Ogden Stiers
9. Loretta Swit
10. Kellye Nakahara
11. Johnny Haymer
12. Jamie Farr
13. William Christopher
14. G.W. Bailey
15. Jeff Maxwell

2. In the Beginning

1. George Morgan
2. a Korean boy Hawkeye took under his wing
3. Maggie
4. September 17, 1972
5. Gene Reynolds
6. Timothy Brown
7. no
8. Sunday
9. Gary Burghoff and G. Wood
10. Odessa Cleveland

3. Capt. Benjamin Franklin Pierce, M.D.

1. Androscoggin
2. *You Never Hear the Bullet*
3. delivering prescriptions for Balanger's Drugstore
4. Vernon Parsons
5. Democratic
6. Boston
7. his work; he's married to it.
8. "the face of every soldier that came through here"
9. carry a gun
10. Father Mulcahy, Radar, and Potter

4. Capt. John McIntyre, M.D.

1. his hat
2. John Francis Xavier McIntyre
3. Boston
4. The pinstripes were horizontal instead of vertical.
5. The map was a World War II army surplus map.
6. 12
7. He was the heating officer.
8. Kim
9. 5 to 1; five parts gin and one moment of silence for the vermouth
10. "You're built, you son of a gun."

5. Nicknames

1. c.   2. f   3. g   4. i   5. a   6. d   7. b
8. e   9. j   10. h

6. Cpl. Walter O'Reilly

1. Eugene
2. put milk on his cereal
3. Linda Sue
4. from the Triple A High School Diploma Company of Delivane, Indiana
5. Protestant
6. Famous Las Vegas Writing School
7. student activities
8. He just saluted.
9. Big Daddy O'Reilly
10. drums, bugle, and piano

7. Lt. Col. Henry Blake, M.D.

1. top left-hand drawer of his desk
2. by snoring
3. a little nativity scene
4. Margaret
5. when the supply line was cut
6. boy
7. a pinstriped suit
8. butterflies
9. $831.71
10. over the Sea of Japan

8. Maj. Margaret ("Hot Lips") Houlihan, R.N.

1. from Klinger
2. in an army hospital
3. $400
4. one eyebrow above both eyes and no neck
5. Lt. Col. Donald Penobscott
6. eighteen years
7. "Over hill over dale, our love will never fail."
8. a cherry branch
9. She'd read that the city of Los Angeles was making one.
10. 20 percent her dad; 10 percent Scully; 10 percent Hawkeye; 3 percent Frank; 1 percent Donald

9. Maj. Frank Burns, M.D.

1. Presbyterian
2. tapioca pudding
3. from his brother when they were kids
4. a schnauzer
5. Your husband, Frank Burns
6. feet and bowels
7. all his clothes
8. 122 out of 200
9. The fragment was from an egg shell.
10. Radar was doing a magic trick; Frank said he knew that one and started to smash his own watch.

10. The Wartime Lovers

1. Thursday
2. "Frank, don't you have enough pain?"
3. His upper lip disappears.
4. her earlobes
5. She said he was a lipless wonder.
6. Bimbo
7. reading and playing footsie
8. a ruby ring
9. Rough and Ready
10. He appllied for a Purple Heart.

11. Hometowns

1. j   2. k   3. g   4. i   5. l   6. r   7. p

8. b   9. m   10. a   11. s   12. q   13. c

14. h   15. e   16. d   17. t   18. n

19. f   20. o

12. Father John Francis Patrick Mulcahy

1. Francis
2. He played poker.
3. boxing
4. Ritz Crackers
5. A nun jumped out of an angel food cake.
6. keeping track of the patients' personal belongings
7. Jesuit
8. While trying to save some POWs he suffered partial deafness.
9. Col. Maurice Hollister
10. saxophone

13. Cpl. Maxwell Klinger

1. Galena and Michigan
2. April 22
3. He's afraid to die.
4. a nose like a hawk
5. orderly
6. Milton Berle, Nelson Rockefeller, and Bishop Sheen
7. 36-24-36
8. "Harbor Lights"
9. Uncle Abdul
10. atheist or, as he said on his entrance exam, Aztec

14. And You Thought We Weren't Watching

1. He said his brother was a boxboy at the supermarket.
2. He arrived at the 4077 in 1952.
3. He rebuilt a motorcycle on the show.
4. She has the nicest legs in Bloomington.
5. Springfield
6. Hawkeye was an only child, or so he said on other occasions.
7. Because Margaret's father appeared in a later episode.
8. Frank's underwear
9. His father is no longer living, so he could not send it to his parents.
10. If his father was a doctor this couldn't have been the only book he ever read.

15. Pranks on Frank

Part I

1. d   2. e   3. b   4. c   5. a

Part II

1. toe tag
2. crate
3. rewrote the Ten Commandments
4. knocked all the walls down
5. fake stock from the stock market

16. Capt. Jonathan Tuttle

1. Berlin Polytechnic Medical School
2. Harry and Frida
3. 1924
4. hair—auburn; eyes—hazel
5. He jumped from a chopper without a parachute.
6. He was in charge of supplementary supplies.
7. Hawkeye
8. Druid
9. Murdock
10. no one; there was no Capt. Tuttle

17. Behind the Scenes

1. Jackie Cooper
2. Johnny Mandel
3. 20th Century-Fox Studios
4. Joyce Robbins and Associates
5. "The Korean Woman"
6. He never directed a show.
7. Walter D. Dishell, M.D.
8. Burt Metcalfe
9. Richard Hooker (aka Dr. H. Richard Hornberger)
10. Mary Kay Place

18. Capt. B.J. Hunnicut, M.D.

1. As he said, "Anything you want it to."
2. Leo Baronaro
3. "Whattaya say, Ferret Face?"
4. argyle socks; he never wears them, but they give him memories
5. He kept exchanging his uniforms for larger ones.
6. three
7. She was his first one-night affair.
8. W.C. Fields
9. May 23
10. 555–2657

19. Col. Sherman T. Potter

1. Doris Day
2. a Hudson
3. His still blew up.
4. tomato juice
5. "Horse hockey!"
6. chipped beef on toast
7. classical banjo
8. Col. Lil Rayburn
9. the field manual
10. Fort Sam Houston

20. Maj. Charles Emerson Winchester III, M.D.

1. the French horn
2. 7½ minutes
3. *Tom and Jerry*
4. Curling and polo
5. Presbyterian
6. He was first in his class.
7. listen to classical music
8. 30 Briercliff Lane
9. bridge, in the Beacon Hill Bridge Society
10. A bullet went through the hat on his head.

21. MISH-M*A*S*H

1. Seoul City Sue
2. old jeep tires
3. Rizzo
4. *MASH Notes*
5. Duluth, Minnesota
6. the dead tree by the latrine
7. "It's a small place."
8. a Studebaker
9. "Is that all you do, bird imitations?"
10. the Lindy

22. Occupations

1. d   2. c   3. f   4. g   5. h   6. a   7. b
8. j   9. e   10. i

23. Col. Flagg

1. No one ever saw him leave.
2. Mr. Big
3. "Personal. A gift for a friend."
4. his virginity
5. communist sympathizer
6. "goldbrickers, pinkos, and fellow travelers"
7. He didn't know the truth; he kept himself in a state of confusion.
8. He trained himself not to laugh. He watched 100 hours of Three Stooges movies and everytime he started to laugh he poked himself with a cattle prod.
9. Sam
10. "If you eliminate the third, fifth, and sixth letters you get *Red's Digest*."

24. Celebrations

1. Radar
2. as King Neptune
3. Come as your favorite nude Pilgrim.
4. Radar, Trapper, and Hawkeye
5. He creamed the corn.
6. He had to find sand for the beach.
7. Operation Bombshell
8. Potter's mortgage was paid up.
9. Col. Potter
10. Everything was dyed red.

25. Strictly Relative

1. Mildred
2. three
3. Honoria
4. Col. Alvin Houlihan
5. yes, two daughters
6. Amos
7. no
8. Peg and Erin
9. Janey and Andy
10. Daniel

26. Double Trouble (1)

1. *The Rooster Crowed at Midnight* by Abigail Potterfield
2. Pink Elephants and Yellow Blackbirds
3. painting and playing horseshoes
4. Cpl. Cupcake
5. March 28 at the Pierre Hotel in New York City

27. The Swamp

1. his mother's and Harry Truman's
2. Moonshine over Korea
3. gin, or as Hawkeye would say, "Chateau Hawkeye, 1951."
4. the Chicago sewer system
5. a dentist's chair
6. a punching bag
7. on the door
8. a helmet for a sink and a metal mirror
9. The Henry Blake Memorial Bar
10. Boston

28. Nurses

1. Clark Gable's
2. Ferguson
3. Nurse Kellye
4. Nurse Able
5. Nurse Cutler
6. They were lovers.
7. Kellye Nakahara
8. Karen Philipp
9. She was in love with Hawkeye.
10. Ballis

29. I'll Drink to That

1. d   2. f   3. g   4. j   5. b   6. c   7. i
8. e   9. a   10. h

30. That's Entertainment

1. two
2. Freddie Nichols
3. played drums
4. The Miller Sisters
5. Brandy Doyle
6. Roads were closed to all vehicles.
7. He fell asleep.
8. "Sweet Molly Malone"
9. Potter
10. Marina and Ellie

31. What's in a Name?

1. Cory
2. Mildred
3. Marion
4. Milton
5. his cousin Billy
6. Molly
7. Leon
8. Col. Flagg
9. Edna
10. dentist

32. What Does It Say On . . .?

1. Medical Supplies
2. No Smoking
3. Loyola
4. Emotionally Exhausted and Morally Bankrupt
5. Dear Giovanni
6. MASH (What else?)
7. The letter I
8. Mudhens
9. For Efficiency and Bugling Above and Beyond the Call of Duty
10. Dear Harry, Who's responsible? Affectionately, A Dissatisfied Customer

33. The Klinger Collection

1. as the Statue of Liberty
2. when a cease-fire was declared prematurely
3. a typewriter ribbon
4. a fur stole
5. Henry
6. his hairy knuckles
7. blue chiffon
8. king of the gypsies
9. his mother
10. Miss Highrise

34. The Operating Room

1. four
2. 121st EVAC
3. Radar Benjamin Franklin Trapper John Henry Kwan
4. Everyone else had the flu.
5. a vascular clamp
6. He operated on an aneurysm—his specialty.
7. They sent for a tub from Sears and sausage casing from Tony Paco's.
8. He touched his nose!
9. rubbing alcohol
10. He saw a grenade inside the soldier.

35. The Sports Page—Page One

1. a gurney race, with nurses as jockeys
2. Father Mulcahy was the only Catholic.
3. a game played with cards, chess, and checkers
4. an inflated surgical glove
5. flies
6. gin rummy
7. twenty questions
8. three-day pass
9. syringes
10. *The American Dream*

36. Radar's Critters and Other Animals

1. e   2. f   3. i   4. h   5. j   6. a   7. b
8. d   9. c   10. g

37. Regular Army

1. initial it to verify that it was his signature
2. They both frown on house calls.
3. "Do not remove this tag."
4. 40 MM Gun; Blake was holding the book upside down.
5. astride the 38th parallel, South Korea
6. AFS 72485 over three small circles and a square
7. Accounting and Finance
8. DA-7 hardship discharge form
9. Fort Dix
10. It was the oath of the president of the United States.

38. Rank Matching

1. d   2. e   3. g   4. c   5. a   6. j   7. h
8. b   9. f   10. i

39. The M*A*S*H-OHOLICS Mindbogglers

1. 20th Century-Fox
2. Lawrence 4864
3. a name Frank gave to Hawkeye and/or Trapper
4. Belvedere Jehoshaphat
5. Calvin
6. (a) Harry Morgan—Gen. Steele and Potter; (b) Charles Aidman—Gen. Korshak and Col. Bloodworth; (c) Dennis Dugan—Pvt. McShane and Potter's son-in-law, Bob Wilson; and (d) John Orchard—Ugly John and Muldoon
7. Fearless Costume Company of Philadelphia
8. 1100:55 hours
9. They are all alias for Col. Flagg.
10. the meeting point to pick up American wounded from the Chinese

40. Let's Go to the Movies

1. Joe E. Brown
2. They are all VD films.
3. *Yankee Doodle Doctor*
4. *State Fair*
5. Horses, cowboys, and horses
6. Box 245, Havana, Cuba
7. *My Darling Clementine*
8. *Ecstasy* with Hedy Lamar
9. He lost a lot of money on that series.
10. *Of Ice and Lice*

41. Where Did They Come From?

1. c 2. e 3. h 4. g 5. j 6. i 7. d
8. a 9. f 10. b

42. Mail Call

1. the Sears catalogue
2. a whip
3. They both had the same name.
4. His wife wanted him to balance the checking account.
5. He sent away for things.
6. a Polaroid camera
7. cookies they made
8. fourth grade
9. B.J.
10. a green parka

43. What Did They Say?

1. incubator
2. handsome
3. operate on yourself
4. drawers
5. Moby Dick
6. Sherm
7. war
8. smile on your face
9. skin
10. register
11. hardens
12. Klinger

44. Which Doesn't Belong?

1. a   2. b   3. b   4. b   5. a   6. a   7. b

8. b   9. a   10. b

45. Violence

1. Frank told Klinger to take off his bandana and he wouldn't.
2. Kid Doctor
3. Frank was accused of raping a female colonel who attacked him. Margaret dropped the charges against Hawkeye.
4. Henry wouldn't let him go home for a while.
5. Lt. Forester
6. The Korean cut Klinger's dress strap.
7. John Ritter
8. The sniper thought the 4077 was MacArthur's camp.
9. Frank; he was the referee.
10. Sgt. Finch punched him because Charles gave his outfit a bad sanitation report.

46. A Name Is a Name Is a Name

1. Padre
2. Beej
3. Pierce
4. Son
5. You Sirs
6. Hawk
7. Hot Lips
8. Henry
9. Colonel Sir
10. anything, especially "My little soldier"
11. Maxie
12. Trap
13. Gentlemen
14. Mother
15. Ma'am Sir or Sir Ma'am
16. the yellow horde
17. Sherm
18. Dad
19. Ben
20. Squirt, Non Com or even Corporal

47. M*A*S*H-RABILIA

1. a Korean/American dictionary, boots, and a straw hat
2. a fishing reel
3. his teddy bear
4. a vase
5. a snowflake paperweight
6. a mustache made out of hair to replace the one that was burned off
7. a riding crop
8. a bedpan
9. a rectal thermometer
10. a gold lighter

48. True or False

1. T   2. F   3. F   4. T   5. F   6. T; he died
as a boy   7. T   8. F   9. F   10. F

49. Who Was That Person?

1. f 　　 2. d 　　 3. h 　　 4. g 　　 5. a 　　 6. c 　　 7. i

8. e 　　 9. j 　　 10. b

50. Generally Speaking

1. Crandel
2. Sherman Potter Hamilton
3. Vi
4. Gen. Collins
5. "He's a pistol."
6. Fort Ord
7. the officers' club
8. They were all generals.
9. in Margaret's bed
10. Potter gave him a case of Preparation H.

51. Local Indigenous Personnel (LIP)

1. f 　　 2. e 　　 3. j 　　 4. a 　　 5. c 　　 6. b 　　 7. i

8. d 　　 9. g 　　 10. h

52. "Dreams"

1. It was a plaid bow tie.
2. riding a horse as a boy
3. Potter operating on Klinger
4. with a magic act
5. his right
6. at his desk
7. becoming pope
8. a wedding dress, which later was covered in blood
9. *The Blade*
10. by train

53. In Living Color

1. yellow or light gray
2. anything but green or khaki gray
3. red or jeep gray
4. orange or off-gray
5. off-blue or almost gray
6. yellow or light gray
7. orange or beer-bottle gray
8. black or black
9. aquamarine blue or navy gray
10. pink or cute gray

54. Female Guest Stars

1. d   2. f   3. e   4. g   5. i   6. h   7. b

8. a   9. c

55. M*A*S*H-AMATICS

1. 42-36-42, same as Mrs. Potter's measurements
2. 34 miles or 54 km.
3. 13
4. 28
5. 175 lbs.
6. 5'5"
7. 97 percent
8. $8.00
9. September 19, 1952
10. 1215 Michigan Street

56. Sing Me a Song

1. c   2. e   3. f   4. d   5. g   6. b   7. a

8. j   9. h   10. i

57. Enlisted Personnel

1. the motor pool
2. Zale
3. Zelmo
4. $71.32
5. Purple Rider
6. Radar, Klinger, Zale, and Igor
7. Luther
8. be a pig farmer
9. Klinger
10. a medic at the aid station

58. Male Guest Stars

1. f   2. o   3. g   4. n   5. r   6. k   7. i

8. b   9. d   10. j   11. c   12. e

13. h   14. p   15. m   16. l   17. q

18. a   19. c

59.   Trading Power

1. the Klinger Collection
2. a case of scotch
3. *Gilda*
4. 100 forks
5. a leg of lamb with mint jelly
6. a dozen cigars
7. a barbecue grill
8. give him a classical record
9. nylons
10. a two-day pass

60. Maj. Sidney Freedman

1. Alan Arbus
2. The discharge said Klinger was a homosexual.
3. He was treating a soldier in a fox-hole, and the enemy attacked.
4. the building of a bonfire
5. Sigmund Freud
6. Theodore
7. at the 4077
8. bus
9. his uniform
10. "Ladies and gentlemen, take my advice: pull down your pants and slide on the ice."

61. "Five O'clock Charlie"

1. He came by at 5:00 every day.
2. six
3. blow up an ammo dump near the 4077
4. Henry
5. Radar
6. Gen. Clayton's jeep was blown up.
7. as Gen. MacArthur
8. "Yes, are you?"
9. They made an arrow out of sheets and iodine pointing to the dump.
10. The ammo dump was blown up by Frank and his gun, and Charlie was seen only once again, in a later episode.

62. Who Said That!

1. Insanity
2. war
3. junior
4. manure
5. psychological
6. Koreans
7. adopt
8. colonel
9. Apples
10. license plate

63. Hawkeye

1. a dictionary
2. He worked for a moving company.
3. a plunger
4. his friend, Tommy Gillis
5. He put a brick in a bedpan.
6. pack a lunch and go watch the nurses hang their wash up to dry.
7. He smelled it.
8. "You tell him, Ferret Face."
9. His father gave it to him after reading *The Last of the Mohicans*.
10. handling the nurses

64. Oops! Wrong Show

1. j   2. h   3. f   4. a   5. g   6. b   7. c

8. e   9. d   10. i

65. Trapper

1. a priest
2. *Field and Stream*
3. Gal o' War
4. 32
5. He painted his skin brown.
6. His girls were growing up and he wasn't there to see it.
7. ten minutes
8. Coolidge
9. "the dirty doctor"
10. over a year

66. Still Strictly Relative

1. Zelda
2. St. Louis
3. She was a concert pianist.
4. Kathy and Becky
5. Laverne Esposito
6. Beacon Hill, Mass.
7. Bubba
8. the name Margaret
9. guns
10. buys and sells import gifts

67. Teasers

1. Radar's lamb; he was going to send it home so the Greeks wouldn't make a meal out of it.
2. Nancy
3. This was an alias Henry used to get Japanese porno prints.
4. Grumpy
5. *Crab Apple Cove Courier*
6. to catch rats
7. because Frank had painted his toenails red
8. claustrophobia
9. It was about Silly Putty.

68. Radar

1. sixty-three
2. O'Brien and Volpe Elevator Shoe Company
3. Radar said Flagg was a CPA.
4. radio headphones with a cloth wrapped around them
5. a paratrooper's scarf
6. The collapsible bathtub they just got in the mail.
7. 12
8. "Stick that horn in your ear."
9. They were black-and-white wing tips.

69. Henry Blake

1. "Rule 1: Young men die. Rule 2: Doctors can't do anything about Rule 1."
2. 34
3. She was Buzz Walinski's date at their college freshman mixer.
4. 36-24-34
5. rare with sugar and brandy
6. "You better behave or I'll have to come back and kick your butt."
7. It was cut up for firewood and it was carried away by a chopper.
8. She wanted to recover the furniture.
9. a second honeymoon
10. orthodontist

70. Alan Alda's Favorite Episodes

1. A visiting female doctor comes to the 4077. Hawkeye wants to get to know the Swedish doctor better. She shows him up in OR with a superior technique and his ego is shattered.

2. Sidney Freedman was depressed, so he came to the 4077 to see how they deal with the pressure. He writes a letter to Sigmund Freud as a form of therapy. Freedman begins to release the pressure in the form of practical jokes with B.J. on Frank.

3. Father Mulcahy writes to his sister the nun. It's right before Christmas. He and everyone else at the 4077 is getting frustrated at being so many miles from home and having to spend another Christmas away from their families.

4. Hawkeye talks Radar into going to Seoul, but on the way Radar is injured. While in the OR Hawkeye has to leave because he is sick from the drinking he did the night before. Radar loses all respect for his idol. Later all is cleared up when Hawkeye pins Radar with his Purple Heart.

5. Hawkeye falls in love with a Korean woman who is doing everything for her family. Her mother is very sick and the house is full of orphans they took in. After her mother dies Kyong Soon packs up her belongings and the children and goes south. All hope for a continued affair has ended.

6. Father Mulcahy comes down with hepatitis. B.J. performs a difficult operation he has to follow the book on. And Hawkeye develops a psychosomatic backache because of a certain doctor's success back in Maine.

7. The whole camp builds a bonfire to release the pressures of war. Meanwhile Sidney Freedman is depressed because a soldier blames him for his injury because Sidney sent him back to the front line.

8–While on their way to the 8063 Margaret and Hawkeye are
9. under military attack. Their jeep breaks down and they have to take cover in a shack. They spend the night together in each other's arms.

10. After talking about a reunion after the war, B.J. gets the idea of not waiting until the war is over. A party is planned for all the families of the members of the 4077. It was a big success, or so they said.

71. Common Ground

1. Both smoked cigars.
2. Both played two different characters on the show.
3. Both had light blue eyes.
4. Both were from California.
5. Their wives were named Louise.
6. Both had private practices at home.
7. Both boxed in college.
8. They had the same blood type.
9. Their fathers were doctors.
10. Both had blood type B.

72. Frank

1. a hernia operation
2. a canary; it didn't sing a note and it bit him.
3. "Frank has the best knowledge of garbage around."
4. Burns Blight
5. It was his mother's wish.
6. with extra fat
7. in the bottle with his appendix
8. $400
9. "America the Beautiful"
10. because he had the biggest tongue

73. The Time Capsule

1. Radar's teddy bear
2. her boots
3. a spark plug
4. her nurses' manual
5. a book, *The Last of the Plainsmen*
6. Henry Blake's fishing lure
7. Nothing; Hawkeye thought of Frank's scalpel, but they didn't want any deadly weapons.
8. a bottle of cognac
9. a black dress
10. his boxing gloves

74. Margaret

1. Darlene
2. She was a nurse.
3. put him in a body cast
4. a fountain made of bedpans
5. "Margaret and I are dating."
6. the death of a man on Christmas; she said he died after midnight rather than before so his family wouldn't have to remember Christmas as the day he died.
7. Hawkeye
8. Hans Christian Andersen
9. leather pajamas
10. no

75. Doctors

1. Robert Alda, Alan's father
2. neurology
3. twelve years
4. He cracked up.
5. Dr. Stanley Robbins
6. The American College of Surgeons
7. eyes, nose, ears, and guitar
8. Richard Paul
9. Capt. Hildebrand
10. University of Illinois

76. What Does It Say on . . . ?

1. "Best wishes, 'Howitzer' Al Houlihan, Knock' em dead, fella."
2. Surgical instruments
3. "Mary had a little lamb, My dog has fleas, Mares eat oats and Does eat oats, and I'll be home for Christmas. Your Loving Son, Queen Victoria"
4. "Give yourself up. You can't win—Douglas MacArthur"
5. "Frank, Dad is not your father. Love, Mom"
6. We Never Close
7. Ernie's All-Stars
8. "To my little shot from her big shot. Your Husband Lt. Col. Alvin Houlihan; Regular Army"
9. Good-bye Radar

77. Klinger

1. El Redondo
2. Q
3. eat it
4. Soon Lee
5. Fort Dix in New Jersey
6. He had to wear a rubber suit and fur coat for twenty-four hours during a heatwave, then Potter would give him a Section 8. He never made it.
7. to be buried in his mother's wedding dress
8. too much swoop in the T
9. she was mugged
10. Arabic

78. Father Mulcahy

1. He was a featherweight boxer.
2. Cathy
3. "Your daughter's pregnancy brings much pleasure to the village."
4. Cardinals
5. in his bathrobe
6. Plato and Gentleman Joe Cavanaugh, the boxer
7. St. Augustine
8. G
9. She has six kids.
10. basketball

79. A Touch of Color

1. red
2. hunter green
3. Green; black; Red
4. white; blue
5. red, white, blue; black
6. yellow
7. blue
8. pink; red
9. blue
10. white

80. B.J.

1. He did; no one else had any money.
2. Blue Velvet
3. hostess
4. his wife, Peg
5. Stanford
6. He had already done it twice.
7. It was his daughter Erin's first sentence.
8. in his right hand
9. Fort Sam Houston
10. the Bronze Star

81. Promotions

1. two: Klinger and Father Mulcahy
2. Corporal captain
3. three
4. He won it in a poker game.
5. four
6. Frank
7. Elmo Hitalski
8. Hawkeye, B.J., and Charles
9. He had to perform a tracheotomy on the boy.
10. Hawkeye

82. Potter

1. Sears Super Slumber Down Mattress
2. VA Hospital in Springfield, Missouri
3. Tex Ritter
4. because it's groundhog day; easy to remember
5. in Tokyo
6. Li'l Abner
7. a Brownie Hawkeye
8. call his wife
9. Methodist
10. That's what his wife called him.

83. M*A*S*H-AMATICS Plus

1. 5¢
2. 5'1"
3. 5
4. 3,976
5. $672.17
6. 10½C
7. 259 miles
8. 42 pompous
9. 16
10. On most occasions it was 5 miles.

84. Charles

1. Tokyo General Hospital
2. by tape recorder
3. shower
4. Pegasus
5. She was a family maid.
6. He was allergic to flowers.
7. silk shirts
8. Klinger saved Charlies's life and in the process broke his own nose and couldn't work. So Charles did.
9. It was never delivered because of a truckers' strike.
10. Dodgers

85. More Nicknames

1. h   2. i   3. f   4. j   5. g   6. a   7. b
8. e   9. c   10. d

86. Cards, Anyone?

1. his mailman
2. a heart flush
3. Radar
4. the Bible
5. Potter, Margaret, B.J., and Charles
6. It was the dead of winter.
7. He whistled loudly.
8. a nurse on the way to the shower
9. a howitzer
10. the mayor of Uijongbu and his brother, the police chief

87. Double Trouble (2)

1. Henderson, Landers, and Flynn; NL7-9000
2. Audrey Hepburn; he has a picture of them together.
3. (1) he was sitting with his feet up and a drink in hand; (2) he was standing next to his tower of tongue depressors
4. Lancaster, Missouri, only 100 miles from Ottumwa
5. About Faces by Margaret Houlihan
6. It was to Hawkeye's dad; the company was Pioneer Aviation.
7. To B.J. she sent the fixings for peanut butter and jelly sandwiches; to Charles she sent nothing.
8. three days in the Argonne Forest
9. Adam's Ribs; the cole slaw
10. He was court-martialed and sent to the VA hospital in Fort Wayne.

88. Hawkeye Pierce

1. *The Joy of Nudity*
2. his father
3. He was a war correspondent from the *Chicago Tribune*.
4. They got drunk together.
5. He sprained his index finger.
6. toilets
7. He shaved off half of B.J.'s mustache.
8. He gave it to Radar.
9. He told them he was married.
10. clean socks

89. Still Singin' a Song

1. c   2. d   3. b   4. f   5. i   6. h   7. e
          8. g   9. j   10. a

90. Rosie's

1. GI Classy
2. Muldoon
3. a Hawaiian sport shirt
4. hot rice
5. Irving
6. $1
7. $8
8. water the booze
9. declare Rosie's an independent nation
10. no one

91. The Sports Page—Page Two

1. most free throws in a row, thirty-two
2. Hawk's Pride
3. his wife
4. on a pole in the center of the compound
5. pole sitting
6. shot glasses
7. a gurney for the table and a surgical mask for the net
8. loser had to chauffeur the other around in a wheelchair
9. the Frisbee and the Hula Hoop
10. bowling

92. True or False

(1) F (2) T (3) T; he grazed his leg (4) T (5) F; Charles did (6) T; he said he did during WW I (7) F (8) T (9) T; long ago (10) True and False. He talked about Sister Angelica and Sister Theresa. Maybe he just forgot what her name was.

93. Stumpers

1. a nurse Hawkeye invented to entice his friend Stan Robbins to come to the 4077 to do plastic surgery on a kid's nose
2. B for boom
3. 1902 Front Street
4. a collapsible bathtub
5. Charlie
6. The States are ahead by fifteen hours.
7. vottz
8. to Tokyo, to San Francisco, then home—wherever that was
9. "If your shoes aren't becoming to you, you should be coming to us."
10. Potter was going 25 mph in a posted 15 mph zone.

94. Hawkeye's Army

1. rest and resurrection
2. crazy in the army
3. He was one of the first in line.
4. the Monument of Stupidity
5. manic depressive
6. He placed an order for sandwiches.
7. to put an end to the war
8. (a) insubordination, (b) disobedience of orders, and (c) impersonating a civilian
9. "The officers' club will open at 0500 hours and remain open constantly."
10. Olivia de Havilland

95. Awards

1. ninety-nine
2. "Dear Sigmund"
3. yes; Gene Reynolds received the Directors' Guild Award for the pilot.
4. fourteen
5. yes; 1977 (Outstanding Continued Performance of a Supporting Actor in a Comedy Series)
6. Telly Savalas
7. McLean Stevenson
8. none
9. 1974. He won one for Best Leading Actor in a Comedy Series and he also won Actor of the Year—Series the same year.
10. (a) Favorite Television Comedy Program, (b) Favorite Male Television Performer (Alan Alda), and (c) Favorite All-Round Male Entertainer (Alan Alda)

96. More Guest Stars

1. j   2. f   3. i   4. g   5. a   6. b   7. c
8. e and k   9. d   10. h

97. Fill in the Blanks

1. brass
2. not intentionally
3. inflamed boil
4. violence
5. your IQ
6. err is Truman
7. decency; indecency
8. I'm ready
9. as little as possible
10. his gold filling

98. Real Teasers

1. A Popeye night-light
2. Col. Baldwin
3. two weeks
4. in the mess tent
5. Margaret and Klinger, but Klinger was married twice
6. pre-Mildred
7. He was promoted to three-star general and sent to the Pentagon.
8. She was his sophomore love.
9. of a stroke
10. no; he was a regular soldier
11. a blanket
12. 39729976 stop
13. an experiment the army was trying, to make crank case oil edible after 5,000 miles
14. twice as long as usual; he flunked out twice
15. because he knew ahead of time what would happen
16. They were the first three names the doctors picked for their pony.
17. his in-laws
18. fifteen
19. Janey Pooh
20. "The Sunburned Fool"

99. What Are You Going to Do After the War?

1. begin her next assignment in a stateside hospital
2. take it easy, get to know his patients, and work in Crab Apple Cove
3. be a pig farmer
4. breed frogs for French restaurants
5. get married and stay in Korea
6. become a semiretired doctor in Hannibal, Missouri
7. work with the deaf
8. be a nurse at the army hospital in Honolulu
9. He said he met a little cookie in Guam at the airport bar and figured what the hell. Then he said he was just kidding.
10. be the head of thoracic surgery at Mercy Hospital in Boston

100. "Good-bye, Farewell, Amen"

1. Chevrolet
2. $450,000
3. Elizabeth Barrett Browning
4. because the sunset was on the wrong horizon that night
5. five
6. There was a tank on the compound.
7. Tokyo and Belgium
8. "If you love someone you got nothing but trouble. So either stop loving them or love them a whole lot more."
9. "Father, I've been wanting to tell you this for a long time—your shirt is on backwards."
10. He wrote it with stones.

101. Riding Off into the Sunset

1. motorcycle
2. chopper
3. jeep
4. garbage truck
5. chopper
6. jeep
7. horseback
8. garbage truck
9. ox cart
10. bus